# Retold Myths & Folktales

African Myths

African American Folktales

Asian Myths

Classic Myths, Volume 1

Classic Myths, Volume 2

Classic Myths, Volume 3

Mexican American Folktales

Native American Myths

Northern European Myths

World Myths

The Retold Tales® Series features novels, short story anthologies, and collections of myths and folktales.

**Perfection Learning®**

Retold Myths & Folktales

# NATIVE AMERICAN *Myths*

by Robert Franklin Gish

**Perfection Learning®**

T 2358794

**Senior Editor**
Marsha James

**Editors**
Wim Coleman
Christine Rempe LePorte
Terry Ofner
Pat Perrin

**Cover Ilustration**
Greg Hargreaves

**Inside Ilustration**
Barry Milliken

**Book Design**
Dea Marks

For information contact
Perfection Learning® Corporation
1000 North Second Avenue, P.O. Box 500
Logan, Iowa 51546-0500.
Phone: 1-800-831-4190 • Fax: 1-800-543-2745
perfectionlearning.com

PB ISBN-10: 1-5631-2315-0  ISBN-13: 978-1-5631-2315-3
RLB ISBN-10: 0-7807-3221-9  ISBN-13: 978-0-7807-3221-6

17 18 19 20 PP 16  15  14  13  12  11

*For My Children and for Their Children.*
*For the Spirit of Story.*
*And for All Keepers of the Word,*
*Now and Then,*
*Young and Old.*

# ABOUT THE AUTHOR

Robert Franklin Gish is currently Director of Ethnic Studies at California Polytechnic State University, San Luis Obispo. He is the author of *Songs of My Hunter Heart: A Western Kinship* (Iowa State University Press, 1992), *First Horses: Stories of the New West* (University of Nevada Press, 1992), and numerous other books and writings about the American West. He is a member of the Cherokee Nation of Oklahoma.

# ABOUT THE ARTIST

Barry Milliken was born in Windsor, Ontario, and grew up on the Kettle Point reservation on the shore of Lake Huron.

After completing an art program in Toronto, Barry worked for many years as a graphic artist.

In 1984 he moved to the small community of Dutton, near London, Ontario. There he is pursuing a career in fine art and illustration.

Barry is a member of the Chippewa Nation.

# TABLE
## OF CONTENTS

**WELCOME** . . . . . . . . . . . . . . . . **1**

**MAP OF NORTH AMERICA** . . . . . . . . . . . . **3**

**CREATION**

The Woman Who Fell from the Sky . . . . . Seneca **7**

The Four Worlds . . . . . . . . . . . . . . Hopi **24**

**ROMANCE**

Scarface . . . . . . . . . . . . . . Blackfoot **43**

Oochigeas and the Invisible Hunter . . . . . . Abnaki **62**

**HEROES**

Saynday Gets the Sun . . . . . . . . . . Kiowa **79**

Two Feathers and Turkey Boy . . . . . . . Seneca **92**

**TRICKSTERS**

Coyote and the Thundering Rock . . . . . . . Sioux **115**

The One Who Sets Things Right . . . . . . . Tlingit **126**

**HOW AND WHY**

The Vision Quest . . . . . . . . . . . . Chippewa **143**

Coyote and Death . . . . . . . . . . . . Caddo **156**

# WELCOME TO THE RETOLD NATIVE AMERICAN MYTHS

These myths and legends of North American native peoples hold within them many truths—truths kept through the ages by the singers and tellers and keepers of the old ways. As such, these stories are the product of countless retellings. And with each retelling, the lessons of long experience are passed from one generation to the next.

We are coming to realize that the Native American oral tradition can help us respect and appreciate the natural world and its many interrelationships—plant and animal, living and nonliving, earth and cosmos.

The native storytellers understand the human need to identify with the natural world around us. The accounts of Coyote, Raven, and Deer included in this collection dramatize our need to know and appreciate our fellow creatures.

It would be most informative to hear what plants and animals think of their human brothers and sisters. But until such a time, we must settle for the insights that myths and legends such as these teach us. From them we can learn about ourselves and about those with whom we inhabit this good, green, and still-living earth.

Robert F. Gish

*continued*

## RETOLD UPDATE

This book presents a collection of ten adapted myths from the native peoples of the North American continent. All the variety, excitement, and humorous details of the original stories are here.

In addition, a word list has been added at the beginning of each story. Each word defined on the list is printed in dark type within the story. If you forget the meaning of one of these words, just check the list to review the definition.

You'll also find footnotes at the bottom of some story pages. These notes identify people or places, explain ideas, show pronunciations, or provide cultural information.

We offer two other features you may wish to use. One is a map of North America on the following page. This map shows the region where each of the myths was originally told.

You will also find more cultural information in the Insights section after each myth. These revealing facts will add to your understanding of the Native American groups represented.

One last word. Since many of these myths and stories have been handed down for centuries, several versions exist. So a story you read here will probably differ from a version you read elsewhere.

Now on to the myths. We hope you discover the mystery and adventure of these Native American stories.

# Native American TRIBES OF NORTH AMERICA

TLINGIT

NORTH

BLACKFOOT

CHIPPEWA

AMERICA

ABNAKI

SENECA

SIOUX

MISSISSIPPI RIVER

HOPI

KIOWA

ATLANTIC OCEAN

CADDO

PACIFIC OCEAN

N

# CREATION

## The Woman Who Fell from the Sky
## The Four Worlds

**M**ost Native American peoples credit the creation of the world to a supreme being. This supreme creator is known by many different names throughout America. Among the Sioux of the central plains, the supreme being is sometimes called Wankan Tanka. The Hopi of northern Arizona call the creator Taiowa.

Animals also play important roles in many creation stories. Indeed, according to some myths, animals and people were brothers and sisters at the time of creation. Only later did the animals change to the shapes by which we know them today.

Many native peoples call the North American continent itself Turtle Island. This is in honor of the turtle who offered to have the island built upon its back. You will meet Turtle in the first myth of this section.

# THE WOMAN WHO FELL FROM THE SKY

## VOCABULARY PREVIEW

Below is a list of words that appear in the story. Read the list and get to know the words before you read the story.

**casual**—effortless; offhand
**commanding**—powerful; impressive
**commotion**—noise
**deftly**—skillfully; with little effort
**distressed**—troubled
**drastic**—extreme; exceptional
**extinct**—gone; dead
**fate**—the future
**gaped**—opened; yawned
**interlocking**—linking; securing together
**jeered**—sneered; mocked
**perish**—die
**resourceful**—clever; skillful
**rivals**—competitors; opponents
**sacrifice**—offering; loss

### Main Characters

**Djuskaha (Twig)**—Turtle Woman's son; Flint's twin
**Othagwenda (Flint)**—Turtle Woman's son; Twig's twin
**Sky Leader**—ruler of the sky world; Sky Woman's father
**Sky Woman**—Sky Leader's daughter; Turtle Woman's mother
**Turtle Woman**—Sky Woman's daughter; mother of the twins

### The Scene

The action starts in the sky world. Then the story moves to the lower world, known as Turtle Island.

# The
# Woman Who Fell
## from the
# Sky

*Sometimes life seems easy, and other times it seems difficult. The Seneca have a story that helps explain why this is so.*

**Y**ou should know that the land and the things on it have not always been the way they are now. Far back, almost before the beginning of time, human beings like us lived high up in the sky. Some people now call that place "heaven," but it goes by other names as well.

In that sky world, there lived a wise and powerful leader. All who lived there followed Sky Leader's orders, and everything seemed at peace. But as the sky people were to learn, not everything was perfect. For one day in those very old times, Sky Leader's own daughter became ill.

"How can this be?" asked Sky Leader sorrowfully. "I'm the most powerful person in all creation. How could this happen to *my daughter?*"

The sky people were greatly **distressed** too. Those who understood the healing arts tried to cure Sky Leader's daughter. But nothing worked. The young woman grew worse, and Sky Leader grew ever more sad and worried. In fact, he became so troubled that he couldn't make wise decisions. He was no longer a good leader for his people.

Now in that sky place there grew a very large, tall tree. This marvelous tree spread its branches over Sky Leader's lodge.[1] At the top of the tree was a great, glowing blossom that lit up the world and perfumed the air. The tree also provided corn that fed the sky people. For this reason, they called it the Corn Tree.

Not surprisingly, the wonderful tree was very important to everyone. In fact, the sky people often dreamed about the Corn Tree and recited their dreams to one another. But one night, a special vision came to one of the sky people.

"The sick girl must lie down beside the Corn Tree," said the voice in the vision. "And then the tree must be dug up. But be quick about it! You must tell her father right away!"

Now these were **drastic** commands. Since the tree was so special to the sky people, it was no small matter to go digging it up. The dreamer wondered what to do.

"The Corn Tree feeds us all," the dreamer considered. "How would we survive without it? But at the same time, the girl must be cured. The Sky Leader grieves so much that he can't lead us as he should."

Gathering all his courage, the dreamer went to Sky Leader's lodge and began to tell him of his vision. He'd barely finished his story before Sky Leader made his decision. He took his frail daughter in his strong arms and

---

[1] The Sky Leader's lodge probably looked like the Seneca longhouse built of bark.

placed her beside the Corn Tree. Then, using all his strength, Sky Leader grabbed the tree and began pulling it out of the sky place where it grew.

Such noise had never been heard before. Sky Leader grunted and gasped. The Corn Tree cracked and groaned. The **commotion** sounded like the thunder we hear today. Indeed, some still say it is Sky Leader we hear when thunder booms and lightning cracks.

Finally, Sky Leader yanked the tree out of the ground. A huge hole **gaped** where the Corn Tree once stood. The hole broke through the crust of the sky world. Sky Leader looked down into it, but the hole didn't seem to have any bottom.

All the same, Sky Leader wiped his hands in satisfaction. "Now my daughter will be cured," he said. "Living without the Corn Tree will be quite a **sacrifice.** But my daughter's life is worth the price."

Meanwhile, the sick girl lay trembling by the hole. She peeked cautiously over the edge. Clouds and empty space were all she could see. The height dizzied and frightened her, so she pulled back and tried to calm herself. She waited to be healed.

Sky Leader sat watching his daughter, also waiting for signs of returning health. But none appeared. Day after day went by, and Sky Leader did nothing but wait. Things grew worse and worse in the sky world.

"Sky Leader, you must come away from here," cried one of his people. "We have no one to watch out for us, to make decisions for us."

"Return to your lodge," begged another. "We need you there."

"And leave my daughter alone?" replied Sky Leader.

"The vision said she would be healed," said another. "Surely that will happen whether you are here or not."

"True," murmured Sky Leader. "There is nothing more I can do for her but wait and hope."

So Sky Leader returned to his lodge, feeling downhearted. The people who had gathered in worried groups also went back to their usual work.

However, Sky Leader's daughter was not left alone. One very angry man remained. No one knows his name, but even so, you probably know who he is. For like disease and other problems, he and his anger turn up in the world today—in fact, we may see more of him now than ever before. Let us call him Angry Man.

"The Corn Tree gave us life!" Angry Man shouted at the Sky Leader's daughter. "That tree fed us! Now it's gone, and it's all your fault!"

"Was it my fault I got sick?" asked the girl with a tired voice. She was still very sick. "Was it my fault that this was the only way to cure me?"

"Bah! That was no true vision!" replied Angry Man. "Even if it *were* true, what good is it to make you well? Now all of us will starve to death!"

Angry Man sputtered and spat. Finally he kicked the girl, and she fell into the sky hole. The girl scrambled and clawed at the earth around the edge of the hole. She tried to climb back up into her world, but she was very sick and weak.

Angry Man kicked and pushed the girl again. She struggled but lost her grip. She only managed to hold onto a handful of seeds from the Corn Tree. Then she fell.

The girl fell through the great hole, through clouds and fog and empty space. Finally she saw water beneath her. The water stretched in every direction, as far as she could see. For at that time, the entire lower world was covered with water.

Now the only living things in that lower world were water animals, such as ducks and turtles and toads. As it happened, a flock of ducks was floating on the water below. One of the ducks looked up and noticed the young woman falling from the sky.

"What kind of bird is that?" one duck asked another. "It doesn't seem to fly quite right. It looks like it's falling."

"Let's go find out," suggested another duck.

The ducks flew to meet the strange creature. As they rose into the air, the birds formed a platform by **interlocking** their wings. Gently, the birds caught the young woman on their feathered backs. But she was heavy, and the birds chattered for help.

Water Turtle and Toad heard the request and swam up to do their share. Turtle allowed the girl to sit on his wide back.

"Who is she?" Turtle asked the ducks.

"Who knows?" answered one of the ducks. "Some unfeathered bird with very poor wings."

The young woman was now coming to her senses and heard this conversation. "I am Sky Leader's daughter," she explained. "You can call me Sky Woman if you like."

And so Sky Woman's life was saved. But the water animals quickly saw a problem. Sky Woman could not swim or fly, so what were they to do with her? She couldn't ride around on the backs of the ducks forever. And there was no room on Turtle's back for her to move about.

"How do you normally get around?" one of the birds asked Sky Woman.

"I walk," replied Sky Woman.

"You *walk?* On what?"

Sky Woman shrugged. "On dry land, mostly."

"Dry land?" asked the bird. "What's that?"

The birds all chattered among themselves, trying to figure out what Sky Woman was talking about. At last, Turtle's deep, **commanding** voice broke in.

"Deep under the water, I have seen mud and sand," he said. "We could use it to build Sky Woman a mound on top of me. This mound would rise above the water—an *island,* we could call it. I believe that's what she means by dry land."

The waterfowl flapped their wings and chattered their approval of this idea.

"But how are we to get any of this mud and sand?" one of them asked.

"Well, I *would* dive down and get it myself," said Turtle. "But Sky Woman is resting on my back."

The ducks chattered worriedly. They knew the depths were full of danger. All the ducks who had tried to find the bottom of the water had vanished, never to return. But brave little Toad spoke up.

"I'll dive to the water's bottom and bring up the mud and sand," Toad said.

And so he did. It took Toad hundreds of thousands of trips. But little by little, he piled load after load of earth on Turtle's back. As the soil piled up, Turtle grew bigger and bigger.

Soon, Sky Woman had room to walk around. Where before she had barely room to sit, now there stretched a vast island. This was how the land we call Turtle Island[2] was created.

On that island, Sky Woman's illness left her, and she was healthy again. She built a shelter like her father's sky lodge. The handful of seeds she had grabbed when she fell quickly took root on the new island. They produced not only corn, but fruit and flowers. A giant tree also grew, just like the Corn Tree in the sky world. It even had a glowing blossom to light the new world.

After living for a time on Water Turtle's big back, Sky Woman gave birth to a daughter. Some called the new child Turtle Girl. When she grew into an adult, Turtle Girl became known as Turtle Woman.

Now Sky Woman and Turtle Woman found many good things to eat on Turtle Island. The wild potato was one of their favorite foods. But they had to dig the potatoes up from the ground. Sky Woman remembered how this was done in her old home and taught her daughter the proper way.

"Always face the West when you dig potatoes," said Sky Woman. "Never face the East."

---

[2] Turtle Island is the name some Native Americanpeoples give to North America.

"But why, Mother?" asked Turtle Woman. "What possible difference does it make which direction I face? The potatoes taste just the same, don't they?"

"I don't know what difference it makes," replied Sky Woman. "It's the way things are done in the sky, that's all. And so it's the way we're going to do things here."

"Very well, then," grumbled Turtle Woman. "I'll do it your way."

But as you know, daughters don't always obey their mothers. One day, Sky Woman noticed that Turtle Woman was with child. She guessed that her daughter had faced East while digging. For you see, when Turtle Woman faced East, the West Wind had created a child within her. Such are the strange ways of the wind.

But the West Wind had not created just one child. Turtle Woman was to give birth to twin boys. And like many ordinary brothers, the twins were **rivals** from the start. Even before they were born, their mother could hear the twins arguing inside her.

"I shall be born first," said one twin to the other.

"No, *I* shall be born first," answered the other.

As it happened, a boy of reddish color was born first. He was called Othagwenda,[3] which means "Flint" in the Seneca language. The second boy was smaller and had a lighter complexion. He was called Djuskaha,[4] or "Twig."

Within moments after they were born, the boys began fighting and arguing. Turtle Woman couldn't control them, so she went to her mother for advice. Sky Woman wasn't pleased.

"We had a peaceful, happy world here," she told her daughter. "But you had to disobey my command and bring two quarrelsome sons into it. If your boys don't learn to get along, who knows what will happen? They could fight and destroy everything! What shall we do now?"

[3] (oˊ thag wenˊ da)
[4] (de jusˊ ka haˊ)

"I don't know, Mother," said Turtle Woman. "I was hoping you could decide."

Sky Woman thought it over for a moment. At last she said, "Which of your sons do you care for most?"

"Oh, don't make me answer that, Mother!" exclaimed Turtle Woman. "They're both my sons. I love them both."

"Even so, both of them can't be allowed to live here. Which do you wish to save?"

Reluctantly, Turtle Woman chose Twig over Flint.

"Very well," said Sky Woman. "Now you must cast Flint into a hollow log somewhere far, far away."

Tearfully, Turtle Woman obeyed Sky Woman's command. She took Flint to a hollow log and sealed him up inside. The boy seemed certain to **perish.**

The years passed, and Twig grew quickly, as little twigs do. He liked to make beautiful bows and arrows to hunt for game. He became quite an expert at such things.

One morning, he left the lodge with a brand new bow and a quiver full of brightly colored arrows. That evening he returned with some game, but his bow and arrows were gone. Twig made a new bow and more arrows in the morning before he left for the hunt. But in the evening, he again returned without a bow or a single arrow.

"Why do you make a new bow every morning?" asked Sky Woman the next morning. "Do you lose it when you're out hunting?"

"No, Grandmother," replied Twig. "I give my bows and arrows to a boy I met the other day. The boy looks just like me. But he lives in a hollow log. The boy needs the weapons, for he has no one to help him get food."

Of course, Sky Woman and Turtle Woman realized that Twig had found his twin brother, Flint. And they realized that **fate** can never be changed. So they went to Flint's tree and brought the abandoned boy home.

The two brothers quickly grew into strong men. Of course, they continued to fight and challenge each other.

One day Flint boasted to his brother, "I bet I'm more creative than you are."

"No way!" replied Twig. "I've already proven that I'm more **resourceful.** You would have starved to death if I hadn't given you the bows and arrows that *I* created."

"That doesn't prove a thing," Flint replied with his fists clenched.

"Well, what have *you* ever made?" **jeered** Twig.

The twins were about to come to blows when Sky Woman interrupted them.

"Why don't you two make yourselves useful, instead of fighting all the time?" she said in a tired voice. "Go explore the island, see what good things you can find."

"That's a good idea, Flint," said Twig. "I'll go in one direction, and you go in the other."

"That's fine," sneered Flint. "And the one who makes the most of what he finds will be the winner."

"You're on!" said Twig.

Now, neither twin knew exactly why he was competing against the other. But each was determined to prove himself better than his brother. So it is with many brothers, even to this day.

The very next morning, Twig walked toward the honored East, and Flint traveled toward the sacred West. Each kept his eye out for creative things to do with what he found. After a time, the twins met each other back at their lodge.

"I've done many fine things out in the West," said Flint.

"And I've done even finer things in the East," answered Twig.

"We'll see about that," replied Flint. "First, let's go take a look at my work."

"That suits me," said Twig. "Why not save the best for last?"

So they went together to inspect Flint's work in the West. Twig couldn't help but be impressed. Everything was big, even if it wasn't particularly comfortable or useful. Flint had made cliffs and ledges and large rocks of amazing shapes. Flint had even created a mosquito that was bigger than both brothers together.

"What's this useless creature?" asked Twig with a laugh.

"A mosquito," replied Flint. "And I happen to be quite proud of it."

"What possible good does it do?"

"Who says it has to do any good? I made it to entertain me, that's all."

"Well, it ought to be able to do something," answered Twig.

"I'll bet it can outrun you," suggested Flint.

"And I'll bet it can't!" said Twig.

Twig took up his brother's challenge and raced the mosquito. The great insect ran like a tornado, raging across the land until it struck a huge tree. With a groan, the tree crashed to the ground.

"This is awful," exclaimed Twig with alarm. "That monster will kill everything in sight—including the people who come after us! Allow me to improve upon this dangerous creation of yours."

With a **casual** flick of his wrist, Twig reduced the size of the mosquito so that it fit into the palm of his hand. Then he blew it into the air, making it fly. And as the insect buzzed away, Twig changed some of his brother's other creations, making them more to his own liking. On the whole, he made everything more comfortable and useful.

Of course, Twig's actions filled Flint with rage. But Flint controlled his temper.

"Just wait, dear brother!" grumbled Flint under his breath. "Soon it'll be my chance to return the favor!"

So the brothers went to the East to judge Twig's work. There Flint found that Twig had made many animals. These creatures were so heavy and downright fat that they could hardly walk, let alone run. This made them easy to hunt and kill.

Twig had also made a sycamore tree with gigantic fruit fit for Sky Leader himself. And he had created many rivers in which the water flowed both ways—half of it upstream and half of it downstream. All in all, Twig's land was a wonderful place to hunt and travel.

"Leave it to you to make life too easy for those who will come after us," grumbled Flint. His red face grew even more flushed than usual with displeasure. "Don't you understand that suffering and hardship build character? Why, nobody will ever have to work here!"

"And how would you improve my handiwork?" asked Twig.

"Well, let's start with these big animals of yours," said Flint. "They won't be able to run fast enough to escape the hunters' weapons. They'll be **extinct** before you know it! Allow me to make a few necessary changes."

**Deftly,** Flint took each of the animals in turn and shook it. Instantly, the animals grew smaller, sleeker, and faster.

"And look at these trees!" continued Flint. "Fruit from these sycamores will fall like rain. The people will be able to pick ready-to-eat food right off the ground. They'll grow lazy. We can't have that!"

With a wave of his hand, Flint replaced the sweet-tasting fruit of the sycamore with worthless balls of seeds. But he did leave the beautiful white bark that makes the sycamore stand out from other trees.

Finally, Flint turned to the rivers that Twig had created. "You want to make life easy, don't you?" said Flint with irritation in his voice. "You don't understand what it means to suffer. You never had to live on your own, did you? You don't know the value of living with difficulty.

"Look at these rivers," continued Flint crossly. "Who'll ever learn to row a boat in rivers that flow both ways? Why, all people will have to do is float wherever they like! That won't do."

With a gesture, Flint made the rivers flow in one direction. Flint then changed other things to suit his own design. By the time he was finished, there wasn't much chance of people having it too easy.

"Now look here!" cried Twig angrily. "What gives you the right to go changing my creations? It's always been like this. You've always bullied me because you were the firstborn."

"And you've always looked down on me like I wasn't as good as you," replied Flint. "What gave *you* the right to change *my* creations?"

Then the rivalry between the twins bore its unfortunate fruit. The brothers began to trade blows. When the fight was over, Flint lay dead at Twig's feet.

That was a sad day. But even now, we can see the outcome of the twins' rivalry in all of nature's ways. Some things seem to make our lives easy, while others make our lives difficult. Good and bad, the twins are with us still.

And what of Sky Woman? She knew what would happen if the twins were kept together. But she also came to realize that, no matter how one tries to change the course of the world, fate always rules in the end.

# INSIGHTS

**B**efore the arrival of Europeans, the Seneca lived in scattered villages in what is now western New York. But the Seneca were not at peace with their neighbors. They and other Iroquois-speaking tribes were at war with the Algonquin and Huron to the north. Sometime in the 1500s, the Seneca united with four other tribes to form the Iroquois League. The League was largely the product of one man—Hiawatha.

Hiawatha originally belonged to the Onondaga nation. As a young man he grew tired of all the fighting among the different tribes. So he called an Onondaga council and suggested several ways to end the wars. However, the Onondaga chief refused to go along with Hiawatha's plans.

Eventually, a discouraged Hiawatha left the Onondaga. He finally met Deganawidah, a Mohawk religious leader who had a dream of uniting all Native peoples. Hiawatha tirelessly traveled among the warring tribes teaching Deganawidah's message. Finally, he was able to form the Federation of the Five Nations and establish peace. Even the Onondaga chief at last allowed his nation to join.

The League's Grand Council was made up of 50 male representatives or peace chiefs. These chiefs were nominated by head women of certain clans. The decision-making process was very democratic, giving all clans and tribes equal say in important affairs.

The Iroquois League split during the Revolutionary War. The Mohawk, Cayugas, Senecas, and Onondagas joined the British. The Oneidas and Tuscaroras fought with the Americans. By the end of the war, the League was crippled.

*continued*

But the Iroquois League certainly left its mark on American history. In fact, some historians believe that the League may have served as a model for the framers of the United States Constitution.

Wooden masks are an important part of Iroquois religious tradition. Also called False Faces, these masks are used as healing aids.

According to Iroquois belief, evil supernatural beings cause illness. The False Faces symbolize spirits that can restore health. In fact, the masks are cared for and fed like living members of the family. Some feel that when they are put on display in museum cases, the masks cannot breathe.

Every year in the spring and fall, the False Faces—worn by members of the tribal medicine society—would visit the homes of the village and "sweep" diseases out of the houses. Grateful villagers sometimes gave the maskers gifts of tobacco.

Afterward a feast was held. Food preferred by the supernatural beings was served. Corn soup and cornmeal mush were two favorites.

Seneca religion teaches that death certainly isn't the end of life. The souls of most people and animals return to the Maker of Souls. However, warrior spirits are said to live in the sky and help protect the living.

The living aren't totally cut off from those who have passed away. Sometimes, ancestors visit the living in dreams. At such times, the dreamer might see his or her dead relatives living in beautiful villages under the earth.

Farming was an important means of survival for the early Seneca. For this reason, six festivals during the year celebrated the stages of crop growth. The first festival was a cleansing ritual. At this time people publicly confessed their misdeeds during the year.

Other festivals were held for planting corn, collecting

the first strawberries, sighting the first corn ears, and celebrating the harvest.

The most important celebration was the nine-day Midwinter Ceremony. At this time, the people thanked the creator for the blessings of the past year and asked for a bountiful new year.

One part of the festivities was a ceremony similar to Halloween. For on the fourth night of the ceremony, the young people dressed as False Faces and roamed the village begging for food.

Today many Seneca are Christians. But thousands still practice the ceremonies of their traditional religion.

# THE FOUR WORLDS

# VOCABULARY PREVIEW

Below is a list of words that appear in the story. Read the list and get to know the words before you read the story.

**barter**—trade; swap
**bustling**—busy
**dismay**—alarm; fear
**finite**—limited; with boundaries
**grudgingly**—unwillingly; reluctantly
**handiwork**—art; creation
**hesitate**—wait; delay
**infinite**—endless space; limitless
**intuition**—inner wisdom; hunches
**lush**—thick with plant life; abundant
**multiply**—increase
**prospered**—succeeded; flourished
**sheer**—steep; vertical
**void**—emptiness
**wayward**—lost; disobedient

## Main Characters

**Sótuknang**—maker of the earth; Taiowa's nephew
**Spider Grandmother**—maker of people
**Taiowa**—the Creator; Sótuknang's uncle

## The Scene

The story takes place in the three worlds that came before the one we know today.

# THE
# FOUR
# WORLDS

*The road of life becomes more difficult as it becomes longer. So taught Spider Grandmother as she led her people from less perfect creations to the one we live in now—the Fourth World.*

**Y**ou may think that this world we live in is the only one there ever was. But long before our own time, other worlds were created and then destroyed.

You see, worlds aren't always made perfectly the first time. When things go wrong, the creators may decide it's best to start all over again. So far, things have gone wrong three times. In fact, three other worlds have each been destroyed to make way for new ones. No doubt that will happen again someday.

In the beginning there were no worlds at all. There was only Taiowa,[1] the Creator. Everything else was a **void,** just endless space. The void was without shape, without beginning or end, without time, and without life.

But in his mind, Taiowa could imagine shape, time, and life. Even though he lived in the **infinite,** he got the idea of a **finite** world. First, he created a nephew named Sótuknang[2] to help him with his work.

"What would you like me to do, Uncle?" Sótuknang asked the moment he was created.

"Let's gather up some of this void, Nephew," said Taiowa. "We'll use it to make universes."

They mixed up bits of the void with some of Taiowa's own being. From this mixture, they created nine universes. One of those universes was to belong to Taiowa. Another was to belong to Sótuknang. The remaining seven were to belong to living things yet to be created.

Sótuknang went to his universe, the one that was to be the First World. This world was named Tokpela,[3] or Endless Space. It was lonely at first. But Sótuknang created Spider Grandmother, a wise and creative soul, to help him make the most of things. Spider Grandmother and Sótuknang looked the world over.

"A very good start," observed Spider Grandmother.

"Still, it's not terribly interesting," remarked Sótuknang.

"Indeed," said Spider Grandmother. "It could use a little life."

So Spider Grandmother took some earth and mixed it with some saliva. She molded the clay into figures and covered them with her cape, which was woven from creative wisdom. She sang the song of creation over the covered figures. When she uncovered them, they had come to life.

Two of these beings were a pair of magical twins.

[1] (ta ē´ ōw a *or* tah´ wah)
[2] (so´ tuk nang)
[3] (tohk´ peh lah)

Spider Grandmother and Sótuknang placed these twins at the poles of the Earth. Their jobs were to keep the world rotating properly. They kept the world stable and solid and the air pleasant and calm. The other beings were trees, plants, flowers, birds, and animals.

Sótuknang and Spider Grandmother looked over their new world, which was now **bustling** with life.

"That's more to my liking!" said Sótuknang with satisfaction. "A very pretty world!"

"Oh, you think so, do you?" replied Spider Grandmother. "And do you want us to stop now, when we could make far more interesting things?"

"What else do you have in mind?" asked Sótuknang.

"You have no imagination," complained Spider Grandmother impatiently. "Don't you understand that the great Taiowa wants a truly special kind of life from us? Stand back and watch."

And Spider Grandmother used four colors of clay this time—yellow, red, white, and black. She molded four forms into the image of Sótuknang. Then she molded four forms into her own image. These were the first male and female human beings on the Earth.

"Oh, yes!" exclaimed Sótuknang with pleasure. "These new creatures are the most interesting of all! But why are they so quiet?"

"Because they have no tongues, I suppose," said Spider Grandmother with a shrug.

"Well, that won't do," replied Sótuknang. "Sooner or later, I'll go crazy with only you to talk to."

So he gave the human beings the power of speech, a different language to each color. He also gave them the ability to **multiply.**

Now that these human beings could talk and listen, Sótuknang was able to give them instructions.

"Always show respect for Spider Grandmother," he told them. "She created you. And of course you should honor me, for I created Spider Grandmother. But you should never forget Taiowa—the Creator of us all. And always act wisely and well toward one another."

And how wise these first human beings were! They had great respect for one another. They understood that the Sun was their father and the Earth was their mother. They understood that the Earth was a living being, just as they were.

They were indeed wise and happy in Tokpela, the First World. Although they were of different colors and spoke different languages, they understood that they were all of one world. They lived in harmony with the plants, birds, and animals, and remembered that they had all come from the Mother Earth. Taiowa, the great Creator, was pleased with Sótuknang and Spider Grandmother's wonderful **handiwork.**

But after a time, many of the people forgot to sing praises to Sótuknang, Spider Grandmother, and Taiowa. They forgot that they were one with the Earth and its plants and creatures. The animals drew away from the people and became afraid of them. Then people became warlike and began to fight one another.

Taiowa looked down upon Tokpela with disapproval.

"So this is what's become of Tokpela!" he complained to Sótuknang and Spider Grandmother. "You've created beings who know no better than to kill each other off— and to kill the Earth as well."

"But what shall we do now?" asked Sótuknang.

"Destroy it, of course," said Taiowa. "Volcanoes raining fire upon the Earth will put an end to it. Once that's done, we can build a new world altogether."

"But we mustn't kill them all!" exclaimed Sótuknang. "Not all the people are bad and warlike."

"That's right," added Spider Grandmother. "The good ones don't deserve to be destroyed."

"Well, save those few if you can," grumbled Taiowa. "But do it quickly, so we can destroy this creation and get on with the next."

So Sótuknang and Spider Grandmother hurried to Earth and gathered together the few wise people who were left. Then they led the people below ground, where the Ant People lived.

The people lived happily underground with the Ant People, while volcanoes rained fire on the world above. The Ant People were generous and shared their food with their human guests. When food ran short, the Ant People just tightened their belts and continued to share with people. That is why ants are so thin around the waist today.

At last the world above cooled off, and Sótuknang created the Second World, called Tokpa,[4] or Dark Midnight. He divided the land and water in a completely different way so that it would not remind the people of the First World.

"Come out now to the Second World," Sótuknang called out to the people living beneath the Earth. "This world is harder than the last, for the road of life becomes more difficult as it becomes longer. But even so, this world has good things to offer."

The human beings came out and gazed upon this new world, and Sótuknang thanked the Ant People for their kindness. Again people lived happily and multiplied. They built homes and villages and made trails between them. However, the animals still stayed away from people.

From the Ant People, the people had learned to make things with their hands and to store food. Now they could trade and **barter** with one another. Eventually, that led to trouble.

The Second World had everything the people needed. But after a time they became dissatisfied. The more goods they traded, the more things they wanted. In their eagerness to get more things, many of them forgot to sing praises to their creators. Many of them began to argue, and then to fight, and then to make war upon one another.

"Another world has gone wrong," complained

[4] (tōhk´ pah)

Taiowa. "There's no solution but to end this one too."

"But what of the few people who still sing the ancient songs and are good at heart?" asked Sótuknang.

"We saved such people last time, and see what good it did us," replied Taiowa.

"But this time they won't go wrong again," pleaded Spider Grandmother. "We promise."

Taiowa **grudgingly** agreed. So Sótuknang again called upon the Ant People to care for the good humans.

When they were all safely underground, Sótuknang called the magical twins back from the poles of the Earth. With no one to keep it in balance, the world spun around and rolled over. Mountains fell into the seas, the water splashed over the land, and the whole Earth froze under solid ice. That was the end of the Second World.

When all life upon the Earth had died, Sótuknang sent the twins back to their positions at the poles of the Earth. The planet began rotating properly again, and the ice melted. Sótuknang was able to work on the Third World, Kuskurza[5]—the last one before our own.

Sótuknang arranged new lands and seas, mountains and plains, and created new life. Then he called the people to come up into their own world again.

Spider Grandmother led the people back up to the surface of the Earth. "You have been given this place by Taiowa," she reminded them. "Live in harmony and do not hurt one another. Try to understand the nature of life. This world is harder than the last, for the road of life becomes more difficult as it becomes longer. So make the best of things, because the next world will be even harder."

First, the people created villages like those of the Second World. But Kuskurza was gray and chilly compared to the worlds they had lived in before. Spider Grandmother taught them how to weave blankets and cloth to keep warm. She taught them to make clay pots and to plant corn. But the pots broke easily, and the corn

[5] (kus kur´ za)

did not grow well. The Third World just wasn't warm enough to live in.

One day a hummingbird came to workers in the fields. They stopped to admire the beautiful creature and asked what it was doing there.

"I was sent here by my master, Masauwu,[6] Ruler of the Upper World, Caretaker of the Place of the Dead, and Owner of Fire. I have been sent to teach you a secret."

The hummingbird then taught the people the secret of warmth. He showed them how to use pieces of wood to make fire. This was a wonderful gift, indeed. The people could gather dried grasses and wood and build fires around their fields. The warmth helped the corn to grow.

One day a fire got away and burned a house down. It was a terrible event. But even so, a wonderful discovery came from it. The clay pots inside that house had become hard and strong. This was how the people learned the secret of firing pottery. Now they could cook their meals and store things in earthen pots and bowls.

Life became more comfortable in the Third World. In fact, the people **prospered.** But their numbers soon became so great that the villages would no longer hold them. So the people created large cities. They created civilization.

Now civilization turned out to be a serious problem. It meant building, building, building things all the time. And if you spend all your time building things around you, how can you remember who you are?

And indeed, most of the people began to forget. The more they concerned themselves with building cities, the less they sang praises to Taiowa, Sótuknang, and Spider Grandmother.

Soon the people began to listen to the evil sorcerers called powakas.[7] These powakas rejected all the old rules of behavior. They did not **hesitate** to use their magical

[6] (mah´ sah wu)
[7] (pō wah´ kahs)

powers to injure those who angered them.

"Forget about Taiowa, Sótuknang, and Spider Grandmother," the powakas told the people. "We're the real creators. We do whatever we like. And if you follow our ways, you can too."

Soon many people were following the powakas and began to behave in terrible ways. The young didn't respect their elders. Husbands and wives sought other lovers. Men left their work in the fields and spent their time gambling. Women joined them instead of grinding corn. Children were given no care, and babies often went hungry.

Most of the people stopped trying to understand the meaning of life. They forgot their creators. Instead, the people came to believe that they had created themselves. After all, hadn't they built these great cities and civilizations?

The more the people forgot their true origins, the more destructive they became. Someone constructed a huge shield out of animal hides. With great effort, he was able to make the shield fly through the air. In a short time, warriors flew on this shield to attack other cities. They killed and wounded countless people.

Soon people in many cities were making such flying shields. Of course, they didn't use the shields for peaceful purposes. They used them to attack one another. So war came to the Third World, as it had to the others. But it was far worse this time. Instead of small villages being destroyed, whole cities went up in flames.

Despite all this destruction, some people still remembered who they were. They still sang songs of praise to Taiowa, Sótuknang, and Spider Grandmother.

These wise people tried to warn their **wayward** brothers and sisters. "Don't you remember what happened to the first two worlds?" said one of the peaceful people. "Taiowa destroyed them."

"Who is Taiowa?" was the only reply.

Meanwhile, Sótuknang and Spider Grandmother

looked on sadly. This time they didn't wait for Taiowa to tell them what to do.

"Taiowa will be angry at what's become of this Third World of ours," said Sótuknang. "There's no point in waiting for his command. If we let this go on any longer, the good people will either be won over to evil or killed. It's best to destroy Kuskurza right away."

"I agree," said Spider Grandmother. "But how are we to do it?"

"I will destroy it with water," replied Sótuknang.

"Water!" exclaimed Spider Grandmother. "But then nobody will be left alive, not even the Ant People. What's to become of the good people still alive?"

But Sótuknang had a plan. First, he commanded Spider Grandmother to gather the good people together at the far end of the world. Then he told her to cut down some tall reeds with hollow stems. Inside each hollow, Spider Grandmother put one of the people. She stocked each stem with some water and cornmeal dough. Then she sealed the reeds shut. Finally, all the good people were ready.

Sótuknang came and sealed Spider Grandmother up in a reed of her own. Then he let loose the waters. The rains came and waves began to roll across the land. Continents broke and sank. Still it rained, and waves higher than mountains rolled across the endless sea.

The people in their hollow reeds could hear what was going on outside. They were tossed about on the waves. They were thrown into the air and dropped back into the water. But the reeds kept them safe from drowning.

Finally everything fell quiet. The reeds floated gently on the surface of the water. After a very long time, even that motion stopped, and the reeds were still.

Spider Grandmother unsealed her own reed. She saw that all the reeds had landed on a tiny piece of land. Before the rains, this had been one of the world's highest mountains. But now only its tip stood above the water.

Spider Grandmother unsealed the reeds of each of

the people. "Bring out all the food that is left," she commanded.

The people brought out their cornmeal dough, which they had been eating since the beginning of the rains. Now they were amazed to discover that there was just as much cornmeal dough as when they started. So they ate eagerly.

"But where is the Fourth World?" the people wondered. "Hasn't Sótuknang created another world for us?"

And indeed, Spider Grandmother wondered the same thing. Here she was, all alone with the few good people left in creation. But there was no sign of Sótuknang anywhere. She wondered if her own creator had forgotten her.

Some birds had survived the storm and landed on that tiny patch of land. Spider Grandmother asked the birds to help them find a place to live. One by one, the birds flew out to search for land. But each bird came back exhausted, with nothing to report.

Next, the people planted one of their reeds in the tiny patch of mud. The reed grew quickly and reached high into the sky. The people climbed the reed and looked out over the surface of the world. But still they could find no land.

Then, at long last, Spider Grandmother heard the welcome sound of Sótuknang's voice.

"Be guided by your inner wisdom," said Sótuknang. "Keep your mind and heart open. Trust your **intuition.**"

Spider Grandmother now knew that she could find the way to the next world. Guided by her inner wisdom, she showed the people how to make boats out of the hollow reeds they had come in. Each person got inside a boat, then pushed off from the tiny mountaintop.

The people drifted for a long time before they saw a rocky island. It was larger than the one they had left, but not big enough for them to live on. After resting, they pushed off again and drifted toward the rising sun.

Soon they saw a big and beautiful land, with trees

growing in grassy fields. As they drew closer, they saw colorful flowers blooming in the sunlight.

"Surely this is our new world!" the people exclaimed happily.

But Spider Grandmother's intuition said otherwise.

"This land is too **lush** and plentiful," she said. "Remember, the road of life grows more difficult as it becomes longer. Our next world will not be as fine as the one which was just destroyed."

As disappointed as they were, the people trusted Spider Grandmother's inner wisdom. They stayed on this land only long enough to cut more hollow reeds and to build rafts large enough to hold entire families. At last, they would be able to travel with their loved ones. Spider Woman also taught them to make paddles, so they could journey more swiftly.

Then the people got on their rafts and pushed off the beautiful land. They journeyed for a very long time before they saw land again. This land was rich and flat, with many trees, plants, seeds, and nuts.

"Surely this is our new world!" the people cried.

But Spider Grandmother shook her head. "No, this is not the Fourth World," she said. "This one is too easy and too pleasant. Here, you would soon fall into evil ways again. Remember, the way becomes harder as it grows longer."

Even so, Spider Grandmother let them stay for a good, long time to rest and eat. The people didn't want to leave this rich and beautiful land. But they trusted Spider Grandmother's inner wisdom. They walked eastward across the island to the far shore, where they made new rafts and paddles. Just when they were ready to leave, Spider Grandmother made a troubling announcement.

"You must go on alone," she said. "I've done all that Sótuknang and Taiowa want me to do for you. You must find your own way into the new world, without my help."

"But how?" asked the people with **dismay.** "You've guided us and taught us. Without you, we would have long since perished. How shall we do without your inner wisdom?"

"You have inner wisdom of your own," explained Spider Grandmother. "Just keep your hearts and minds open, and follow your intuition. Then you'll come to no harm."

Reluctantly, the people thanked Spider Grandmother and set out on their own. They paddled hard for many days to the east and north. Finally they saw land.

This land rose high above the waters and stretched from north to south as far as they could see. Their hearts and minds told them that this was a good land—not as easy and pleasant as the world they had lost, but good enough to start again.

"This is the Fourth World!" they cried to one another.

But they could find no place to land their rafts. The shore of this land was a steep wall of cliffs and mountains. At first they went north, but the wall of cliffs rose higher and higher. Then they went south. Again they faced a **sheer** wall of mountains.

The people then followed Spider Grandmother's example and listened to their inner wisdom. Their intuitions told them to drop their paddles and let their boats drift. Soon their rafts were caught in a gentle current which carried them to a sandy beach. It was their entryway into the Fourth World—the world where we live now.

As the people stepped out onto the beach, they heard the voice of Sótuknang speaking to them from across the land.

"Look back the way you came," said Sótuknang.

The people looked back across the water and saw the islands upon which they had rested during their journey.

"Those are the tops of the mountains of the Third World," said Sótuknang. "But that world is no more."

And as the people watched, each of the islands sank into the water, one after another.

"I had left them as stepping stones for you," Sótuknang said. "Now I have washed away even the footprints of your journey. Now all your cities lie on the bottom of the sea. Now all your flying shields and other inventions are sunk beneath the depths. The people who forgot to sing praises to the Creator have drowned. But if you remember your creators, if you keep the meaning of your wondrous entrance into this world, these stepping stones will one day emerge again."

Today there is nothing left of the Third World. We live in the Fourth World. It is called Túwaqachi[8]—which means World Complete.

[8] (tu wa qa´ chi)

# INSIGHTS

The Hopi (which means "peaceful") are a Pueblo tribe of the southwest. *Pueblo* is a Spanish word that means "village." The Spanish so named the Hopi and other southwestern tribes because of the distinctive villages that they built out of stone or adobe.

It is believed that the Hopi culture is one of the best-preserved Native American cultures of the United States. This may be due to the fact that the Hopi resisted European influences. In 1680, for example, the Hopi destroyed Spanish missions on their territory. They then migrated and built new villages in more remote areas.

Hopi villages now standing are grouped along three peninsula-like extensions of the Black Mesa in northern Arizona. These extensions are known locally as First or Eastern Mesa, Second or Middle Mesa, and Third Mesa.

The village of Oraibi—on the Hopi Third Mesa—is probably the oldest continually lived-on site in the United States.

It is said that some Hopi children got lost while traveling through a canyon. They were able to survive only by eating berries.

Eventually eagles saw the children and took pity on them. They brought food to the lost children and protected them from harm.

The children began to think of the eagles as their own people. They even started to imitate eagle calls. Then one morning, the children were turned into eagles.

From then on, whenever Hopis caught a small eagle, they brought it home and washed it. Then they gave it a doll, just as though the eagle were a child.

Hopi religion is centered on superhuman beings called *kachinas*. The kachinas embody the spirits of living things and the souls of ancestors. They also possess power over nature, especially the weather.

There are more than 500 kachinas. Each one has a particular spirit and fulfills a certain function. For example, the *Hon* or bear kachina is said to cure the sick. And the giant *Chaveyo* makes sure that no one breaks the rules of conduct. However, the most important kachinas are those that provide rain for the villagers' crops.

One tradition states that the kachinas once lived on the earth and danced in the villages to bring all-important rain. But the people became evil, so the kachinas left the villages and refused to return. However, the kachina spirits allowed the people to impersonate them. So the Hopis dress as kachinas and dance and sing their requests.

Hopi children are taught to respect the kachinas. The kachinas visit all the children in their homes. They demand that the girls grind corn and the boys catch mice. A few days later the kachinas return, demanding their "food."

If the supply is not enough, the kachinas threaten to kidnap the children. Kachinas will also threaten to eat a naughty child. So the Hopi children learn early not to take the kachinas lightly.

The children also learn about the kachinas from dolls. These are usually carved from the roots of cottonwood trees, and some are elaborately decorated with feathers, claws, or animal skins.

The Hopi myth of the four worlds is kept alive in places called *kivas*. A kiva is a sacred underground chamber. It is the place where Hopi men transform themselves into kachinas.

*continued*

The coming of the Hopi into this world is remembered by a *sipapu*—a small hole in the kiva floor. It symbolizes the place of coming into the world at birth and leaving it at death.

Each kiva also has a hole in the roof. This symbolizes the hole in the sky where the people entered the Fourth World.

Some Hopi games have special meaning to the community. For example, a game called *shinny* is important because it is played at the beginning of the growing season.

Shinny is played by two teams of boys. They play with a buckskin ball filled with seeds. It is said that if the ball doesn't break after four days of playing, the crops will not be plentiful.

Spinning tops is another game played for the good of the community. Tradition holds that the humming of the tops will summon winds that bring clouds filled with rain.

# ROMANCE

## Scarface
## Oochigeas and the Invisible Hunter

Love overcomes all obstacles, especially in myths. Native American storytellers enjoy tales of lovers finding each other despite the odds.

Native American romance stories often emphasize the fantastic. A maiden marries the morning star, or a young man travels to the land of the sun. Yet these stories teach very important human lessons as well.

In these stories, the hero or heroine is often flawed or imperfect in some way. For example, in both the stories that follow, the main characters have scars on their faces. However, in the course of their quest for love, their inner beauty shines through for all to see.

# SCARFACE

# VOCABULARY PREVIEW

Below is a list of words that appear in the story. Read the list and get to know the words before you read the story.

**banished**—exiled; sent away
**compassion**—understanding; tenderness
**crestfallen**—sad; discouraged
**dejected**—disheartened; depressed
**grotesque**—ugly; displeasing
**kinship**—family; relatives
**marveled**—wondered; was in awe
**notion**—idea; thought
**queried**—questioned
**rebellious**—wild; unruly
**transfixed**—enchanted
**unsightly**—ugly; unpleasant
**verge**—edge; brink
**vibrant**—dazzling; bright
**welled**—came to the surface; rose

## Main Characters

**Feather Woman**—Morning Star's wife; Poia's mother
**Morning Star**—Sun's offspring; Feather Woman's husband; Poia's father
**Poia**—also called Star Boy; son of Morning Star and Feather Woman; his name means "Scarface"

## The Scene

The action starts in a Blackfoot village on the northern plains. Then the story moves to the sky world and finally returns to the village.

# Scarface

*His mother and father had named him Star Boy. But the Blackfoot people called the homeless boy Scarface.*

*And with time, even he forgot his true name. He forgot, that is, until he fell in love.*

**T**he shadow that **kinship** casts is long. It reaches into the regions above and the places below. It gives us a sense of who we are. And great sadness can come to those who forget their families—so a young Blackfoot man named Scarface found out.

Our story begins before Scarface was born. On a hot summer night, two young sisters of the Blackfoot tribe left their cowskin lodge[1] to sleep in the cool air by the river's edge. The sisters awoke just before dawn. In the east they could see the morning star[2] rising from his sleep along the edge of light and dark.

The youngest sister was so taken with the beauty of the star that she spoke to him. "Oh, beautiful star of the dawning light, no man on Earth compares with you. Please be my husband."

The older sister laughed. "What foolishness!" she said. "Do you really think a star can hear you, much less want to marry you?"

The younger sister was surprised. It really hadn't occurred to her that her prayer might be foolish. "You don't think the morning star can hear my prayer?" she asked.

"You'd better hope it can't!" replied the older sister. "Because if it can, the whole heavens must be laughing at you. You'll have a hard enough time finding a good man to marry without looking to the stars."

The younger sister blushed with embarrassment.

"Oh, it really is foolish, isn't it?" she said. "But the truth is, I love this star more than any man alive. Promise you won't tell anybody."

"What, and have everybody think I have a half-wit for a sister?" said the older sister with a laugh. "Your secret is safe with me."

But the older sister was not true to her word. She told everyone that her younger sister had fallen in love with a star. The whole family made fun of the young sister's romantic **notion.**

The young girl laughed too, but she still couldn't forget the beautiful morning star. Several mornings later, she went to the river's edge to draw water. A young and glorious man was standing there, waiting near the spot where

---

[1] The Blackfoot lived in tipi-like dwellings, sometimes called lodges.
[2] The morning star is the name of any one of several planets (Venus, Jupiter, Mars, Mercury, or Saturn) that rises just before the sun.

she and her sister had slept.

"Greetings, maiden of the morning," said the young man. "I am Morning Star."

The young girl looked at him with disbelief. "Yes, and I'm the spirit of this river," she said.

"But I'm telling you the truth!"

"Of course you are. How nice to have met you. Now kindly leave me alone."

The young man sighed deeply. "Can it be that I've found the wrong woman?" he said. "I could swear it was your voice I heard, asking me to marry you."

"Young man, I don't know what village you're from," replied the girl. "But I know a joke when I hear it. And I've been hearing nothing but jokes ever since my people found out I was in love with the morning star. So kindly go find another girl to tease."

"So it *was* you!" exclaimed the young man. "What can I do to prove to you that I'm really Morning Star?"

"You can't," said the girl. "So don't waste your time and effort."

But the young man took a yellow feather from his headdress and gave it to the young woman.

"Close your eyes and hold on to this," said the mysterious young man.

The girl took the feather. Suddenly a strange sensation **welled** up within her. She felt herself lifted upward by the wind—softly, magically. Her head spun and her feet became numb. But soon she landed on what seemed to be solid Earth, although it felt much softer.

Then the young man took the feather from her hand and whispered in her ear. "Open your eyes," he said. "You are now Feather Woman, wife of Morning Star— just as you wished!"

Feather Woman looked around the sky which was her new world. It was beautiful! Everything was more intense and **vibrant** than on Earth. Colors were brighter. Distances were greater. The air was clearer.

Many animals roamed the sky world. Death was

unknown in that place. When animals were killed on a hunt, they were restored to life the very next day.

Morning Star introduced his bride to his parents. And what parents! His mother was Moon and his father was Sun, the lord of the sky world.

Together Sun and Moon built a lodge for the young couple and placed it close to their own dwelling. Then they went back to roaming the heavens as they usually did. Sometimes Morning Star traveled with them, and Feather Woman was often alone.

As with most societies, the sky people had one taboo.[3] When Feather Woman first arrived, Morning Star told her, "You can go anywhere in the heavens. But you must not touch the large turnip that grows in the center of the sky. This is a sacred turnip. And to touch it would mean disaster."

"But surely one turnip is like any other!" exclaimed Feather Woman. "We have turnips back on Earth, and we pick them all the time. What makes this one so sacred? What a strange request!"

"It's not a request," insisted Morning Star. "It's a command. So kindly obey me, and don't even touch the turnip. I don't think that's too much to ask."

"Very well, then," said Feather Woman. "I was never overly fond of turnips, anyway."

After a time, Feather Woman and Morning Star became parents to a fine baby boy. They named him Star Boy. As her son grew up, Feather Woman had someone to keep her company. These were good times for her.

Feather Woman had always obeyed the taboo about the great turnip. But one morning she went on a walk alone. Her route took her straight to the sacred turnip.

Was it by accident that she followed that path? It is something of a puzzle. Maybe Feather Woman was in a **rebellious** mood. Or perhaps she was just curious. Or maybe she was tired of following Morning Star's orders.

---

[3] A taboo is a religious rule. People fear being punished by a supernatural force if they break the taboo.

By this time, she was beginning to regard him as just an ordinary husband.

For whatever reason, Feather Woman touched the turnip. Nothing happened.

"Why, what a fool my husband is!" she exclaimed. "He told me disaster would strike if I so much as touched this turnip! Why, the thing is harmless, perfectly harmless."

The turnip was, indeed, quite huge, and Feather Woman was tired from hours of walking. So she leaned against the turnip. Still, nothing happened.

"How odd!" Feather Woman mused. "I've been away from Earth so many years, I actually rather miss the taste of cooked turnip. Why, this one here would make many good meals."

So she picked up a stick and used it to dig around the turnip's base. In a matter of moments, Feather Woman had dug around the entire plant. She was trying to uproot the sacred turnip! But the turnip was too large to budge. Looking around for help, Feather Woman saw two cranes flying overhead.

"Friendly cranes," called Feather Woman, "fly down here and help me dig up this old turnip. Don't ask me why. I just have to do it, that's all. But I don't have the strength. Can you help?"

Well, you know cranes. They're helpful creatures by nature. And they can dig and pull with their long beaks. Soon all of the dirt around the base of the turnip was loosened. Then, with a great tug, Feather Woman pulled the sacred turnip out of the ground.

Where the turnip once grew was now a large hole. With her heart racing, Feather Woman looked down into the hole. What she saw there filled her with astonishment.

Below her stretched the great prairie—the home of the Blackfoot people. She saw her own village, with the smoke rising from the tents. She could even see people she knew, all of them going about their daily affairs. And there was her own sister walking down to the river for water.

Of course, seeing the family that she had forgotten made Feather Woman homesick. She watched and watched, **transfixed.** She didn't even notice Morning Star standing behind her, on the **verge** of tears. For he knew the price his wife now had to pay for breaking the law.

"Oh, my wife!" he exclaimed. "What a terrible thing you've done!"

Feather Woman looked at her husband with surprise. "But why is it so terrible?" she said. "You told me something awful would happen if I touched the turnip. And now—look here!—I've dug the whole thing up, and nothing has happened!"

"Oh, but something has," replied Morning Star. "Look into your heart. It's torn between Earth and Sky. You long for Earth again, but you could never be happy there. Nor can you be happy here. You no longer know which is your true home."

Feather Woman wept, knowing what Morning Star said was true.

"I am powerless to help you," continued Morning Star. "You are **banished** from the sky forever."

Sadly, Morning Star called two Star Spiders and had them weave a strong web between the heavens and the Earth. Feather Woman took Star Boy into her arms and began to climb down the web to the Earth. The journey didn't take long. In fact, some who saw Feather Woman and Star Boy descend that night thought they had seen a shooting star. They **marveled** at the sight.

At first, Feather Woman was happy to see her own people again. She began to teach them all that she learned in the sky world. She told them about the death and rebirth of the sky animals and how the dead are given new life in the spirit lands of the sky.

Then Feather Woman told them of her husband and their son, Star Boy. And as she spoke of her husband, she was overcome with sorrow. She could feel her heart breaking. Then she remembered Morning Star's words.

"Look into your heart," he had said. "It's torn between Earth and Sky."

Finally, suffering from bitter sorrow and longing, Feather Woman died. Of course, the people mourned Feather Woman's death, and they honored her with a proper burial. But soon, her memory faded from the people's lives.

These were sad times for Star Boy. Left without a mother or a father, he wandered homeless among the Blackfoot people. He wore tattered clothes and was forced to beg for food and shelter.

To add to his troubles, a strange and **grotesque** scar appeared on the side of Star Boy's face. Each year the scar grew larger and redder in color. People said that it looked as if a bear had clawed the boy's face.

People began to call Star Boy by another name. They called him Scarface—or in his language, Poia.[4] Soon, Star Boy forgot all about his sky family. He accepted the name of Scarface.

In time, Poia grew to be a young man. And as young men do, he fell in love. He fell for the most beautiful girl of all the Blackfoot people. Or so he thought, for such is the way of lovers.

She was the daughter of a chief. Of course, many handsome and rich young men danced for her.[5] Each one hoped that she would pick him for her husband. But she turned them all down.

One day, a group of such handsome men saw poor Poia walking though the village. "Why don't *you* dance for the chief's daughter?" one of the young men said with a laugh. "You're so handsome and rich, surely she will pick *you* to marry."

Poia looked at them scornfully.

[4] (pō ē´ a)
[5] As in many cultures around the world, dance is a part of courtship among Native Americanpeoples.

"I won't dance for her," he said.

"And why not?" asked another of the young men.

"Because I have nothing fine to wear."

All the young men laughed loudly at this.

"What a fool you are!" said another of the men. "Why, with that face of yours, your clothes are the last thing you should worry about!"

"Listen here," said Poia. "I only said I wouldn't dance for her. Even so, I *will* ask her to marry me."

The men laughed at Poia's words. But that very evening, he walked to the river where the women collected water. There he waited until the young woman approached. As she came nearer, Poia turned his face, trying to hide his **unsightly** scar.

The girl smiled. "I have seen you in the village," she said. "But you turn your face when I approach. Why don't you ever speak to me?"

Then, as if a dam had burst, Poia expressed his deepest feelings. "I am poor," he said, still keeping his face to one side. "My face is flawed. But I love you. If I were not known as Scarface, I would ask you to share my name, to become my wife. I avoid you because I long for you. Those are my feelings."

"I have seen the scar on your face," replied the beautiful girl with a smile. "So you don't have to look away from me. I see beyond the scar, and I know you to be good and handsome."

Encouraged by her kind words, Poia looked squarely at the young woman. "Would. . .would you marry me, then?"

"I cannot," she replied. She looked away toward the sun as it set in the west.

"Because I am poor and scarred?" asked Poia in despair.

"No," replied the girl sadly. "I am forbidden to marry any man."

"Why?"

"The Sun spoke to me in a vision," said the woman.

"He said that I must not marry, that I am his."

Poia was **crestfallen.** For a moment, he had thought he could be happy. But now he was sure that he would spend the rest of his days alone, a wanderer among the people.

The woman was aware of Poia's sadness. "But if I could marry," she said kindly, "I would marry you. You are not like the rest. With you there is something special."

The girl's words were like sunshine brightening the darkness of Poia's life. He suddenly remembered some of the stories his mother had told him—stories of Moon, Morning Star, and Sun. It seemed to Poia that somehow he knew those powerful beings.

In a flash he spoke again, this time with new energy and hope.

"I will seek out Sun's lodge and ask him for your hand."

"If you can find Sun and if he grants your wish, then I will marry you," said the woman. "But Sun must also remove the scar from your face as a sign. That way I will know that you have been successful."

Poia was happier than he had ever been. He found new meaning in his life. But his joy soon turned to despair. Poor Poia had no idea how to find Sun's lodge.

But he was determined to try to win this beautiful woman. So he prepared a sack of pemmican.[6] Then he set out to search toward the west, where Sun disappeared each evening.

Poia crossed prairies and climbed mountains. He lost himself in thick forests. And he asked all the people he met if they knew where Sun lived. He even asked the animals.

One day Poia met a wolf. Wolf cocked his head to the side and **queried** Poia. "You're far from your home. What brings you to the forest?"

"I seek the lodge of the mighty Sun," replied Poia.

---

[6] Pemmican is a food made of dried meat and berries.

"Can you show me the way?"

"I have traveled far, but I have never seen Sun's home," said Wolf. "Have you asked Bear? He is wise in these matters."

So Poia sought Bear. But Bear didn't know either. Poia asked Eagle. He asked Raven and Beaver. Poia even ran by Coyote's side for some distance to learn what he knew. But not one of the animals could tell Poia how to find Sun's home.

One evening Poia was tired and discouraged. His food had run out, and the forest seemed endless. "I'll never find my way!" he sighed as he threw himself to the ground.

"*Never* find your way?" asked a small voice. A wolverine poked his head out from behind a rock. "Oh, it can't be as bad as that. Where are you going? Perhaps I can help."

"I seek the home of Sun," said Poia. "I love a woman who belongs to him. I must find him to ask for her hand."

Wolverine broke into laughter.

"Why do you laugh?" asked Poia.

"Because I know where Sun lives," replied Wolverine.

"And is the secret so funny?"

"No, not at all," said Wolverine, calming himself. "I don't know what got into me. Come, let me show you where it is."

Wolverine waddled up a nearby hill, and Poia followed. A marvelous sight greeted Poia when the two reached the top of the hill. Before him stretched a body of water that seemed endless.

"There," said Wolverine as he pointed where Sun was sinking into the ocean. "It's across the water. There you will find Sun's home."

Poia staggered.

"But how am I supposed to get there?"

"Well, that's your problem, isn't it?" said Wolverine, breaking into laughter again. Then Wolverine went away.

With a deep sigh, Poia fell down to rest. He watched

the sinking Sun. "I'll never find a way to your world!" he whispered, knowing Sun couldn't even hear him. "The water is too wide. I'll never have my heart's desire. I may as well die here. Without her, there is no meaning to my life!"

As Poia sat miserably on the shore, a majestic swan flew overhead. "What are you doing here?" asked Swan. "You're a long way from your people, aren't you?"

"I seek Sun's land," sighed the **dejected** young man. "But I have no way to cross this water."

"Nonsense!" said Swan. "Look at me, brother! Do I look like I haven't flown greater distances than that? And isn't my back broad enough for a young man like yourself?"

"You can take me, then?" asked Poia, his hopes rising again.

"Nothing easier!" said Swan. "Climb on my back. I'll fly you across to Sun's home."

Poia's eyes shone with new energy. "You are my special helper," he said, pulling himself onto Swan's back. "I won't forget you."

Poia rode on Swan's back all night long. When they reached the far shore, Swan circled to the ground and allowed Poia to step off.

But as soon as Poia set foot on the land, Sun himself approached.

"What's this?" grumbled Sun. "A mortal! And an ugly one, too, with a scar on his face! How did you get here? It was Swan, wasn't it? That rascally bird is always bringing mortals here. Well, be off with you! Leave here at once!"

"But I've traveled so far to get here!" exclaimed Poia.

"And a lot I care!" replied Sun. "Mortals aren't allowed here."

"But how am I to get home?"

"The way all the mortals before you did. You'll swim."

Poia looked out across the huge expanse of water. His heart sank. He was sure that all the other mortals who'd tried to swim back had sunk to the bottom of the ocean. And surely he would too. But how was he to argue with Sun himself?

But Poia was in luck. For Morning Star came along at just that moment. He recognized his son.

"Wait, father Sun," said Morning Star. "This is Star Boy, my son. He is now a man. Don't send him back so soon. He's our kin, our relative."

Sun suddenly beamed with surprise. "Then this boy is my very own grandson!" he said. "This is an unexpected pleasure!"

Poia was welcomed into the land of Sun, the sky world he had known as a child. He hunted with Morning Star. He shared feasts with Moon and Sun and the sky people. But Poia still dreamed of the beautiful Earth girl. He just was afraid to approach Sun with his request.

One day while Poia and Morning Star were hunting, seven large and angry birds approached them. It seemed that one of their kind had been killed and somehow not restored to life. Now they planned to raid the sky world and kill everything they found.

Poia understood their loss. "I, too, have lost a loved one," he told the birds. "My mother, Feather Woman, died and was never restored to life. I had to learn to live with the sorrow."

Although they were still angry, the birds were comforted by Poia's words. They thanked him and went their way in peace.

Morning Star heard Poia's words to the birds. He was very impressed with his son's wisdom and **compassion.** And he was grateful that Poia had saved the sky world from much destruction.

Morning Star told Sun what Poia had said and done. Sun was so impressed that he called for Poia.

"Grandson," Sun said, "I understand that you have served my people. For this, you may ask for any reward you want."

Poia hung his head. "I ask for nothing, sir."

Sun frowned. He knew perfectly well that Poia was in love with the beautiful Earth girl. But how was he to give her to Poia if the boy wouldn't speak his mind?

"Come now, my boy," said Sun impatiently. "You're young, you have dreams and wishes, and I'm in a rare frame of mind to grant them. Don't miss your chance."

"I thank you, Grandfather," Poia responded, gathering all his courage. "I do have a request. I ask you if I can marry the beautiful Earth girl—the one which you have claimed. And. . . " Poia paused. "It would please me greatly if you could remove the scar from my face."

Sun rose and approached Poia. Sun's radiance made Poia's eyes squint. Then the boy felt a pleasant warmth pass over his face. He actually felt his scar fade away, leaving his skin smooth and clear.

Morning Star then stepped forward and spoke in a kindly way to Poia. "Return to Earth, my son. And marry the beautiful Earth girl. But before you go, I have some things to give you. I want you to share them with the people."

Morning Star handed Poia a magic flute, sacks of grain, and many special herbs and roots. Then he showed Poia the movements of a dance.

"You must remember this dance," ordered Morning Star. "It is called the Sun Dance. It will give strong medicine and power to the people."

Finally, Morning Star gave Poia a pair of moccasins. "Wear these magic moccasins. They will lead you along the glowing dust of the Wolf Trail. That trail will guide you to Earth. Go. Marry the Earth girl. But then return to the skies to hunt again with me."

The Wolf Trail is what we call the Milky Way. Poia followed it for a very long time before it brought him to the Earth again.

Few recognized Poia as he walked among his people on the way to claim the beautiful Earth girl. His face was as smooth as that of a baby. And he wore fine clothes and many rich ornaments. The young men dared not laugh at his splendor.

Poia told the people of his adventures and arranged to show them the steps of the Sun Dance. There was a great gathering of the Blackfoot peoples when the first Sun Dance was held. It gave the people much purpose, hope, and strength of heart.

Poia then approached the young woman. His heart was beating anxiously.

"My love, do you remember me?" he said. "Do you remember how you once promised to marry me?"

"Yes," said the woman with a smile. *"If* you got permission from Grandfather Sun."

"And so I have," said Poia. "My healed face proves it."

"Indeed it does," said the woman.

"But of course, it's been a long time since then," said Poia cautiously. "You may have given me up for dead. If you have found another man, I'll try to understand."

The woman's face broke into a smile. "I'll marry you, Poia," she said. "I've thought of no one else but you."

Great was Poia's happiness. Still in his magic moccasins, he took his new bride and traveled back along the Wolf Trail into the sky. And there they live to this very day with Sun, Moon, and Morning Star.

On cloudless nights, look long and hard just beyond the Milky Way. You will see Poia and his wife walking through the heavens with their many children and relatives.

# INSIGHTS

The Blackfoot were at the height of their power in the mid-19th century. They were known by their enemies as the most warlike people on the northwest plains.

Although the Blackfoot honored bravery in battle, they were also fun-loving. They enjoyed welcoming guests into their lodges and then hurling mock insults at them. It was the host's duty to prevent the joking from going too far. Sometimes the host family would pretend to fight in front of guests. The fun would end with everyone wrestling with the confused visitors.

The Sun Dance is the Blackfoots' greatest religious festival. A medicine woman plays the lead role in the ceremony. Before the event begins, she fasts for several days to purify herself. Then she leads the camp to the site of the dance. There a medicine lodge is partially built, with an altar put inside.

Those attending the ceremony sing a series of prayers and songs while the medicine woman puts on her sacred garments. She always wears a digging stick like the one Feather Woman used to dig up the sacred turnip. Before the medicine woman leaves the lodge, the altar is destroyed. This symbolizes another occurrence in "Scarface"—Sun's removal of Poia's scar.

The medicine woman and her assistants then face the sun, and pray for the health and well-being of the tribe. After this, the medicine lodge is completed.

In the next part of the ceremony, men dance outside the medicine lodge for four days without eating. Then comes the most dramatic part of the Sun Dance. Young men step forward and perform painful acts of self-torture.

*continued*

Each man inserts sticks through the skin of his chest. Ropes suspended from a pole are tied to the sticks. Then the men lean back and revolve around the pole. Men generally recover from this, but their scars never disappear.

Though the sun was important to the Blackfoot, the sun wasn't the creator. That honor goes to Napi, or Old Man. According to the Blackfoot, Old Man created not only the world but everything in it.

Napi made the earth from a ball of mud. He also made his wife, Old Woman, from a lump of clay. Though the two were equal, Old Man insisted that he should have the first say in everything. Old Woman agreed, as long as she could have the second say.

Together the two of them designed humans. Old Man wanted to place the eyes one on top of the other on the face. But Old Woman, who always had the second (and final) say, decided that they should be on either side of the nose.

Next Old Man tried to put ten fingers on each hand. But Old Woman said no, that was too many. That's why people have four fingers and a thumb.

All went well until the question of death came up. Old Man dropped a buffalo chip in the water. If the buffalo chip floated, Old Man said, then people would live forever. It floated. Then Old Woman, who always had the second say, stepped in. She picked up a rock and said that if it sank, then people would die. Of course, the rock sank. Old Man and his wife agreed it was better that way.

The Blackfoot were divided into three main tribes—the Pikuni (or Piegan), Kainah (or Blood), and Siksika (or Blackfoot). The three tribes lived independent of each other. But they spoke the same languages, had the same customs, and fought the same enemies. Today they have merged into one tribe.

No one knows for sure how the Blackfoot got their

name. Some believe that the Cree Indians first called them by this name. Perhaps the Blackfoot once dyed their footwear black. Or maybe their moccasins were covered with black earth or ash when the Cree named them.

# OOCHIGEAS AND THE INVISIBLE HUNTER

# VOCABULARY PREVIEW

Below is a list of words that appear in the story. Read the list and get to know the words before you read the story.

**adorned**—decorated
**berating**—scolding; blaming
**bidding**—commands; requests
**bounty**—rewards; generosity
**cordially**—politely; in a friendly manner
**desperation**—despair; sorrow
**majestic**—great; splendid
**meddle**—interfere; stick one's nose in
**proposal**—offer
**recognition**—praise; credit
**regrettable**—unfortunate; unhappy
**retorted**—replied cleverly or sharply
**reverently**—with respect
**singe**—burn slightly; scorch
**taunted**—made fun of; mocked

## Main Characters

**Abit**—Oochigeas' older sister
**Oochigeas**—youngest of three orphan sisters; her name means "Scarred One"
**Oona**—Oochigeas' eldest sister
**Sees All**—Team's sister
**Team**—invisible hunter; brother of Sees All

## The Scene

The story takes place in the land of the Abnaki in northern Maine and southeastern Quebec.

# Oochigeas and the Invisible Hunter

*Oochigeas was quiet—the sort of young woman everyone over-looked. But under her simple nature, Oochigeas had great strength and determination. Here's the story of how she found her courageous spirit.*

**T**his is a story from the land of the Abnaki—a land with many lakes. On the edge of one of those lakes was a certain village where three sisters lived.

Now the two oldest girls, Oona and Abit,[1] were quite beautiful. Or at least they were beautiful in their own eyes, for they were both proud and selfish. The two older sisters thought only of what they wanted. They constantly ordered their younger sister around and treated her unkindly.

[1] (oon´ a) (ā ´bit)

The youngest sister, on the other hand, was shy by nature and plain in appearance. The poor girl even began to believe that she was ugly. Of course, her proud sisters did nothing to change her belief. They had no concern for her happiness.

Their parents were dead. The three orphans survived by making pottery and trading it to the hunters for food. Of course, the two older sisters kept the easiest work for themselves. Oona, the eldest, would weave twigs and bark into the shape of a pot. Then Abit, the middle sister, would line the woven form with clay.

When the clay was dry, it was removed from the form and given to the youngest sister to finish. This meant she had to paint the pot and then bake it in a hot fire. She was always leaning deep into the fire. As you might guess, she would often **singe** her hair. And now and then she would burn her hands, arms, and even her face.

Sometimes Oona and Abit even bumped into her as she leaned into the oven. "Why are you always in the way?" they would say, as if it were the youngest girl's fault. As time went by, the cruel older sisters began calling her Oochigeas,[2] which means "Scarred One."

Oochigeas accepted her sisters' rude behavior and their cruel ways. As the youngest sister, she had no choice. But secretly, Oochigeas was happy about one part of her job. She was glad that Oona and Abit left her the most creative part of making the pots—the painting.

In fact, it was Oochigeas' painted designs on the pots that everyone admired. Of course, the older sisters took all the credit for the designs and never gave Oochigeas any **recognition.**

Oochigeas' **regrettable** situation was not a secret. Indeed, the great chief, Glooscap,[3] had seen for himself how the older sisters took advantage of Oochigeas. But he did nothing.

---

[2] (oo chē gā´ as)
[3] (gloos´ cap)

Now, Glooscap had an assistant named Marten who carried out the great chief's **bidding.** And Marten, too, saw how Oochigeas was treated. One day Marten approached Glooscap, looking puzzled.

"You look confused, Marten," said Glooscap. "What troubles you?"

"I'm your assistant," began Marten in a quiet voice. "I do what you request of me. And most of the time, I don't complain."

"What are you getting at, Marten?" asked Glooscap.

"Well, you are my chief, and you treat me fairly and kindly. You never take advantage of me."

"This is true," agreed Glooscap. "Maybe that's why I am chief."

"So why do you let injustice fall on others?" asked Marten, his voice rising.

"Would you tell me what you're talking about?"

"I speak of Oochigeas," said Marten. "Her sisters treat her so cruelly, yet we just stand by and watch. Why haven't you done something? I, for one, am ready to teach those evil sisters a lesson. Just give me the word."

"So *that's* it," said Glooscap. "Kind Marten, I do feel sorry for Oochigeas. But it's not always wise to **meddle** in such matters. Oochigeas is both patient and good. But for the Abnaki, it is more important for a person to be courageous. Let's wait and see what sort of courage this young woman shows."

So, to Marten's disappointment, Glooscap chose not to help Oochigeas.

In the meantime, another family was about to enter into Oochigeas' story. In a lonely spot on the far side of the lake lived a brother and sister. The brother's name was Team,[4] which means "Moose." You see, the moose was the special animal that gave Team strength and power.

Now, Team had a great gift, one that no one else had.

[4] (teem)

He could make himself invisible. As you can imagine, this was a wondrous power. Yet Team never used it for his own advantage, as a more selfish person might. Instead, he lived a simple life in complete harmony with nature.

Team's sister was named Sees All because she saw beyond the visible world. She took special care of Team. For when Team made himself invisible, Sees All was the only one who could see him.

Team's invisibility made him a very great hunter. He needed no bow and arrows. He would approach an animal like the wind. Then, after whispering a prayer, he would **reverently** take the animal's life. His own special animal, the moose, had taught him great respect for those of the wild.

Team's life, however, was lonely. He soon felt a strong need for a wife. He needed someone other than his sister to share his **bounty.** Team especially wanted to share the stories of nature's mystery and beauty. Sees All, too, was lonely.

So, Sees All went to the lakeside village and made an announcement.

"You have all heard of my brother, the great hunter Team," she said. "You know of his kinship with the moose and the other forest animals. But my brother also needs human friends. He needs a wife. I am here to say that he will marry the first woman who can see him."

The people gasped with alarm. They all knew the great hunter Team by another name—the Invisible One. None of them had ever seen him.

"What woman can expect to see the great Team?" they asked.

"None except the very bravest," answered Sees All. "To all others, he will be nothing but the rustling of leaves in the wind. But to the brave woman I am looking for, he will be quite visible. And for her, he will make a fine husband and provider."

Since they had never seen him, none of the people in the village knew whether Team was tall or short, heavy or slim. But they were sure that he had great power. They knew he would always provide food and shelter for any woman he chose to be his wife.

So all of the women in the village were eager to accept Sees All's **proposal** on behalf of her brother. To marry Team would be the honor of a lifetime.

There must have been about as many unmarried women in that village as there are kernels in an ear of corn. Each and every one of those women went to Team's lodge. But try as they might, they never spotted a trace of the invisible hunter.

All this time, the three sisters had been very busy making pottery. But word of the proposal finally reached them. Of course, the announcement created a stir in the household. Oona and Abit immediately began arguing with each other. Each one wanted to be the first to go look for Team.

"I am the eldest, sister," Oona proudly told Abit. "It's my right to go first."

"I'm younger and more beautiful than you are, sister," replied Abit. "Surely this man of magic will prefer my special charms."

The two sisters could not agree who should go first. So they decided to go together. In their selfishness, they didn't even think about Oochigeas. To them, Oochigeas was a homely, unattractive girl, and no man could possibly be interested in her. Surely she couldn't compete for a great hunter's love.

Oochigeas listened and watched while Oona and Abit dressed. They put on their finest robes and placed brilliant bracelets on their arms. Beautiful combs **adorned** their hair.

After Oona and Abit set out in search of Team, Oochigeas returned to her oven. She was working on a pot that was quite different from the others she had made. On it, she was painting the design of a man and a woman.

Oochigeas had poured her heart into this design. Now

she looked at the young couple on the pot. A feeling stirred inside her.

"What is it about this design that fascinates me so?" she asked herself.

Meanwhile, the prideful sisters made their way to the invisible hunter's lodge. As they approached, Sees All greeted them **cordially.**

"No doubt, you have come about my brother," said Sees All. "He will return soon from his hunting. Why don't you wait here by the side of the lake? That way you can tell me when—or *if*—you see him."

Just then, Sees All looked over the lake. "Here comes my brother now," she said. "Do you see him coming across the lake?"

The sisters strained their eyes and saw a canoe moving toward them. But to their surprise, the canoe was empty. At least it appeared empty to Abit and Oona. Team was paddling his canoe directly toward the lodge. But to the ordinary person, he was invisible.

The sisters were overcome with panic. Yet they refused to admit that they couldn't see the great invisible hunter.

"Why, yes, I see your brother," said Abit with a shaky voice. "He is quite. . . quite handsome."

Not to be outdone, Oona cried, "Yes, I see him too. And he is waving at me!"

"No, he's waving at me!" protested Abit.

"At *me,* I tell you!"

Of course, Sees All could tell that the two sisters saw nothing. She knew that they spoke out of **desperation,** as liars often do. But she decided to test them further.

"Tell me, sharp-sighted sisters," she continued. "What is my brother's shoulder strap made of?"

Now Abit figured that the shoulder strap had to be made of either rawhide[5] or willow twigs. So she took a wild guess.

---

[5] Rawhide is untanned animal skin.

"Rawhide," she said boldly. "Plainly, his shoulder strap is made of rawhide."

"No," said Oona, "it is woven of willow twigs."

Such obvious dishonesty angered Sees All. So she decided to measure out a small punishment to teach the sisters a lesson.

"Come to our lodge," she said with a smile. "We'll prepare a meal for my brother."

Each of the sisters assumed that she had given the correct answer. So they excitedly followed Sees All into the lodge. There they helped prepare a meal. When they were finished, Sees All looked toward the doorway.

"And here comes my brother now!" Sees All said. "Welcome, Team. I await you with food and two guests."

The dishonest girls saw nothing, not even a fluttering of the hide which hung across the doorway.

"Take my brother's load of meat," Sees All told Abit. Abit gasped, for she saw no meat. Nothing that Team was wearing or carrying could be seen by an ordinary person.

Then suddenly, a slain deer dropped right on Abit's feet! She screamed out in pain and fright and ran limping from the lodge.

"Take off my brother's wet moccasins," Sees All told Oona. "Then place them by the fire to dry."

Oona had no idea what to do. She saw nothing. Suddenly, a pair of wet moccasins flew out of nowhere and slapped her hard on the face. Shaking in fear, Oona ran from the lodge as fast as she could.

"Ah, those were fine-looking girls," said Team, watching after them. "Yet so false. Will I never find a worthy wife?"

"Oh, yes," Sees All said firmly. "Don't lose hope. You will have an honest wife—and a brave one too. I'm sure of it. Just have patience."

Back at the village, the two sisters started **berating** each other.

"If you hadn't lied to her first, we would have gotten away without being humiliated," said Oona angrily.

"Oh, so it's all *my* fault!" **retorted** Abit.

Just then, Oochigeas approached to see what all the noise was about.

"And what are *you* looking at?" Oona yelled at her.

"Why don't you get back to work?" added Abit. "And mind your own business!"

Oona and Abit took out their rage by screaming and throwing things at their sister. Poor Oochigeas was stung by her sisters' harsh treatment. With tears in her eyes, she ran away from their lodge. She went back to her place by the fire, where she worked on her pottery.

There she sat looking at the special pot she had been working on. She picked it up and gently ran her fingers over the design. True, the man and woman on the pot were merely painted figures. But even so, Oochigeas felt very close to them somehow.

As she gazed at the pot, her thoughts turned to the invisible hunter. "Maybe I should try to see this Team," she said to herself. "But he is such a **majestic** hunter—a brother of the moose. Certainly he wouldn't be interested in a simple and scarred pottery-maker like me."

Then Oochigeas heard her sisters arguing again. She didn't much care to go back to the lodge.

"What have I got to lose?" Oochigeas asked herself. "Even if I can't see Team, perhaps he will allow me to serve him. A brother and sister living alone in the wilderness must need a helping hand. Anything is better than living here."

So Oochigeas drew up her courage. Ignoring her fear, she prepared to meet Team.

Of course, Oochigeas had only rags to wear. But there were beautiful white birch trees all around. So she gathered up pieces of bark. Then, with long stems of grass, she sewed the bark into a dress and leggings.

These handmade garments weren't very comfortable. They felt harsh against Oochigeas' skin. And they made a crackling sound when she walked. But Oochigeas was sure that they had a natural beauty of their own.

Her sisters thought otherwise. When they saw Oochigeas they howled with laughter.

"Where are you going, you homely, fire-scarred girl?" **taunted** Oona. "Surely you don't expect to see the Invisible One."

"I don't expect anything," replied Oochigeas quietly. "If I fail to see him, I will ask to serve him."

And so, with much boldness, Oochigeas threw back her shoulders and proudly walked away. In a short while, she found her way to the lodge where Team and Sees All lived.

"I've come to see Team," Oochigeas said simply when she was greeted by Sees All.

Sees All looked at Oochigeas, with her scarred face and rough clothes. "What courage it must have taken for her to come here!" thought Sees All. Then, taking Oochigeas by the hand, she said, "Come, let us go to the lake."

At the edge of the water, Sees All asked, "Tell me, young one, what do you see out on the water?"

"I see an empty canoe, that is all," came Oochigeas' honest answer.

"Look again. Look hard, dear girl," urged Sees All.

Oochigeas cast a second look out to the lake. This time she thought she saw something in the canoe, but she wasn't sure. Oochigeas felt a wave of fear. But she gathered her courage and looked harder. There *was* something there. She could see a man in the canoe.

"Yes!" she gasped. "Now I see him plainly."

"And what is his shoulder strap made of, girl with the scarred face?"

"Why, why, can it be? It is fashioned out of the rainbow and all its colors. Oh my, such a beautiful rainbow strap! Such a proud and handsome hunter! It can only be Team—the Invisible One."

"Yes, it is Team," said Sees All. "Now hurry back with me to our lodge. For you must prepare yourself to greet him when he enters."

So Sees All took Oochigeas back to the lodge and prepared a fresh bath of spring water for her. Then she provided her with the softest dress of tanned doeskin and gave her a magic comb made of porcupine quills.

To Oochigeas' amazement, the spring water healed all her scars. And one pass of the magic comb restored her hair. It became long and glistening and as black as the crow's wing.

Oochigeas was transformed. Her outward form was as beautiful as her inward person. All her honesty and goodness now came shining through.

At last, Team entered the lodge. Oochigeas gazed at him in wonder. Suddenly she felt as if she had seen him before.

Then she knew. The painting on the pot, the two lovers—they were Oochigeas herself and Team! The design she had worked on so hard and had loved so much was now coming to life. And when Team looked at Oochigeas, he knew she was to be his bride. For he, too, had seen such a picture in his own mind.

The two just stood there face to face, gazing at each other. They looked deep into each other's eyes, feeling their hearts meet and unite as one.

Sees All saw this, too, and smiled. She knew that all their lives would now unfold in peace and in beauty. The three of them would live together and make a wonderful home.

So Oochigeas had not only found a husband, but a new sister as well. And perhaps most important of all, she had found herself. She was happy at last.

In time, Glooscap heard of the marriage of Team and Oochigeas. "It was as I guessed," he said to Marten. "She was a girl of courage, you see. Through courage she was able to see what no one else could see. Through courage, she found happiness. This you should remember, my friend. This you should remember."

Such are the stories of love and courage, the invisible and the visible, in the land of the Abnaki.

# INSIGHTS

**A**bnaki means "People of the Dawn." The name seems appropriate because the traditional homeland of the Abnaki is the southeast portion of Quebec—the place of the sunrise.

An Abnaki origin myth states that the people were created by Tabaldak, or "the Owner." First Tabaldak made people of stone. But he didn't like these beings, so he broke them into pieces.

Next Tabaldak tried using wood from living trees. He liked these people much better and let them survive. According to tradition, these wood people are the ancestors of the later Abnakis.

Tabaldak also created other beings called quasihumans, or almost-humans. These terrifying creatures were the people's enemies.

Several almost-humans lived underwater. These dreadful creatures included a giant lizard and a great serpent. Another was the swamp spirit. This spirit tried to lure children to its swamp and drown them.

However, the most awful almost-humans didn't live in water. They were the Forest Wanderers, a race of giant cannibals. Anyone spotting a Forest Wanderer's tracks in the woods would turn at once and go the other way. A Forest Wanderer could only be killed by cutting it into tiny pieces.

The Abnaki who follow the old ways still live in extended families. This means that parents and children, as well as grandparents, aunts, uncles, cousins, and in-laws, live together.

*continued*

Each family identifies with a guardian animal, such as the bear, the beaver, or the raccoon. The Abnaki like to identify themselves with the animal's good qualities. For example, a family with a bear as its guardian is known for its strength.

Sometimes more than one family share a guardian animal. These families then form a family band, similar to a clan. In earlier times, family bands often hunted together.

It is still a custom for family bands to help each other in times of need. Thus every member not only has his or her own blood relatives to rely on, but also a larger, "adopted" family.

In the days before European influence, the Abnaki lived mostly by hunting and gathering. They did some farming as well, but the growing season was short. Therefore, the most reliable food sources were the animals they hunted.

The hunting season usually began sometime in late winter. At this time, all of the villagers except the old and sick left for the hunting territories.

The boundaries of a hunting area were generally marked by streams or rivers. Each territory was controlled by a specific family band.

It was customary to hunt only one-fourth of the territory at a time. This was wise use of the land's resources, since the hunted animals in each quarter had time to repopulate. Rotating the territories was wise for another reason as well. In the off seasons, the animals would get used to living with humans in peace. Thus the animals became partially tame and easier to hunt.

In traditional Abnaki belief, each individual is made up of two parts—the body and the vital self, or spirit. Both parts are important for survival. However, the vital part can leave the body and move around on its own for a short time. It can also communicate with other spirits.

If the vital self doesn't return to its body, the person can get sick. In such cases, the person's family tries to bring the vital self back with prayers and food. If the vital self stays away too long, the person could die.

The Abnaki also believe that dreams are the result of actions experienced by the vital self when it travels. A person who dreams of doing improper things might feel guilty. However, a person who dreams of performing great or kind deeds can take pride in behaving so well.

# HEROES

### Saynday Gets the Sun
### Two Feathers and Turkey Boy

**H**ero myths and stories are common throughout the world. Indeed, most cultures define themselves through their heroes.

Native Americanmyths and legends honor heroes who are not only brave and strong, but resourceful as well. They also value the hero who is willing to sacrifice for others.

To these heroes, "winning" is not the goal. The emphasis of the heroic quest is to seek good for all. In the two myths that follow, the heroes do just that. They use their strength and wit to help their people.

# SAYNDAY GETS THE SUN

## VOCABULARY PREVIEW

Below is a list of words that appear in the story. Read the list and get to know the words before you read the story.

**air**—outward appearance
**assumed**—took up; adopted
**complimented**—praised
**considerable**—plenty of; substantial
**frantic**—wild; violent
**impressions**—affects; influences
**ingenuity**—skill; ability
**jostled**—bumped
**lamented**—cried; moaned
**loped**—ran; jogged
**mused**—pondered; thought
**orb**—ball; planet or other celestial body
**pensive**—thoughtful
**sauntered**—strolled
**trek**—journey

## Main Characters

**Deer, Fox, and Magpie**—Saynday's friends
**Saynday**—hero

## The Scene

The story takes place in a land with no sun.

# Saynday Gets the Sun

*Long ago,
the Other Side people captured the Sun
and kept it for themselves. No doubt those
selfish people thought they could keep the
bright ball of light forever. But Saynday and his
friends had news for the Other Side people.*

**S**aynday[1] sat all by himself in the cold and dark. That was the only place Saynday could sit, because on his side of the world there was no Sun.

Now Saynday was a very **pensive** person. He thought about such things as light and darkness. And because he had no company, he talked out loud to himself.

[1] (sayn´ day)

"Light would reveal new truths," he said. "When you *see* things, you know them differently. That's what is sad about this darkness. We are left without truly knowing our world."

Saynday could hear his own words. But he could see nothing at all.

"It would be nice," he said, "to see your words. In the chill of a frosty dawn, as the sun gives light and warmth, you could see who your words touch. You could see the **impressions** your words leave on the faces of your friends."

Saynday realized something that disturbed him very much. "What friends?" he said with alarm. "This darkness is so thick, I haven't been able to meet new friends. I'll have to do something about that."

So Saynday began to walk about, searching for friends. Not far away there was another conversation going on. This was a real conversation, for Fox and Deer had bumped into each other in the dark. Of course, they began talking about the surrounding gloom.

"Does this night go on forever?" asked Deer, who kept looking over his shoulder. Deer was a nervous animal.

"I've heard that there once was light enough to see to the end of the earth," replied Fox with an **air** of knowledge. "Imagine that!"

Just then the two animals were interrupted by the **frantic** sound of flapping wings. They could tell it was their friend Magpie from the screech that followed. She was upset because she had narrowly missed running into a nearby tree trunk.

"This darkness *has* to end!" announced Magpie. "I can't see well enough to fly!"

"We were just discussing that very problem," said Fox. "Do you have any suggestions for brightening up this place a bit?"

"No," snapped Magpie. "Who do you think I am, some sort of magician?"

As the animals talked, Saynday happened along. He was glad to find someone else to talk to.

"What's on your minds, friends?" Saynday asked.

"We don't like living this way, always in darkness," squawked Magpie. "Animals can't live in darkness. How am I supposed to fly if I can't see? How am I supposed to be happy if I can't fly?"

"How am I supposed to hunt?" barked Fox.

"How am I supposed to jump over fallen branches?" **lamented** Deer.

"I'd like to be able to see too," said Saynday. "I want to be able to make new friends. And you know what? It's selfishness that keeps us from seeing."

"Selfishness?" called out the animals at the same time.

"How is that so?" asked Magpie.

"Those that live on the other side of the world have captured Sun," answered Saynday.

"Sun?" asked Deer. "What is that?"

"I bet it's that great light that once filled our world," offered Fox proudly.

"You're right," replied Saynday. "It's a bright ball of fire and light. And it's held captive on the other side of our world."

"How curious," Deer said. "How did it get there, and how does it spend its time?"

"Sun was given to our world by the keeper of all," explained Saynday. "The Keeper thought that the light and warmth would be shared by everyone. But those on the other side stole it and kept it for themselves. I say we should go and borrow it back!"

"Don't you mean *steal* it?" asked Fox, with a smile in his voice.

"No, Fox," replied Saynday. "It's wrong for anyone to take something and keep it to themselves."

"I have an idea," said Deer. "We could keep Sun for a while. Then the people on the other side could have it back for an equal amount of time. That seems fair to me."

"Sure," replied Saynday. "Then plants and animals could live and grow equally on both sides."

"But how can we get this sun?" asked Magpie with alarm. "Surely the people on the other side must guard it carefully."

"Let's think this over," **mused** Saynday. "Tell me, each of you, just how far can you run—or fly?"

"I can run almost forever," boasted Fox. "Call it a long, long way."

"I can jump with **considerable** grace and run for a while," spoke Deer in a soft but proud voice. "Call it a short long way."

"I can fly and then dip and glide, and then fly some more," chattered Magpie. "Call it a long short way."

"I can only run several miles," said Saynday. "But then I have to rest." He thought hard for a few minutes. "Hm," he said at last. "I have an idea that might work. Are you all willing to take a risk?"

"Yes, we're with you," responded the three animals.

"Each one of you will play an important part," said Saynday. "And you must do just what I ask of you."

The animals agreed to follow Saynday's orders. They all wanted to get Sun back so their side of the world would be warm and bright again.

"Fox," said Saynday, "you're a sly fellow. Go to the village on the other side of the world. Use your **ingenuity** to *borrow* Sun from the villagers."

"You can count on me," said Fox. "This is a mission worthy of my talents. I'll leave immediately."

"Deer will meet you in a certain place," Saynday continued, "and you will pass Sun to him."

"With pleasure," smiled Fox.

As Saynday gave further instructions to the others, Fox began his journey. It was so dark he couldn't see behind him or before him. But he ran eagerly into the darkness.

After a long time, Fox began to make out a thin line of light. He ran toward it. And soon the light grew so bright that he had to squint his eyes.

He saw a high hill before him. He **loped** to the top and stood there panting. His long tongue hung out of the side of his mouth. But he was smiling. He'd made it into the lighted half of the world.

Fox could see! But he had been in the dark for a long time. At first, his eyes stung and watered from the light, and everything looked like a blur. He thought he could make out figures running and throwing things. Fox shook his head and looked again. Slowly, his vision began to clear.

Suddenly, Fox could see the whole world spread out before him. His eyes focused on a strange sight. Some of the Other Side people were throwing spears at a ball that rolled about in a large field.

But wait! It wasn't a ball at all. They were trying to spear Sun.

Excitedly, Fox crept down the hill to take a closer look. The Other Side people formed two long lines that faced each other. First, one line would roll Sun, and the opposite side would try to spear it. Then that side would roll Sun even faster, and the first side would take its turn trying to spear it.

Fox suddenly had an idea. He trotted toward the team that seemed to be losing. Then he yelped out, "I'm for the losers and wish them all good luck."

The words inspired the captain of the losing team, and he flung his spear directly into Sun. This scored him a point, and his team won the round. So the captain walked over to Fox.

"You bring us good luck, my friend," said the captain. "You have my gratitude. With you as our mascot,[2] we shall always win."

As you might expect, the captain of the other team was upset. He stormed up to the first captain and the Fox.

"This intruder has ruined our game," he yelled, his

---

[2] A mascot is an animal adopted by a group for good luck.

face twisted with rage. "I demand that this—this *dog* be chased away. If not, I'll toss my spear at him."

"*Dog?*" sputtered Fox. But then he had an idea. Instead of getting angry, he smiled. "I just wanted to make things even," he said. "I think both of your teams are equally skillful."

"Hmph!" said the captain whose winning streak Fox had stopped. But he didn't look quite as mad as before. Fox saw that his plan was working.

"This game you play looks interesting," Fox continued to the two team captains. "I'd like to learn to play myself. Would one of you be willing to teach me?"

"Certainly," replied the friendly captain. "The rules aren't hard to learn. However, mastering the game will take a lot of practice."

"Then it looks like I'll be around for a while," said the sly Fox.

And indeed, Fox stayed with the Other Side people for quite some time. Besides learning their game, he got to know all about the people themselves. He learned their names. He visited all their dwellings. He even entertained their children. He became a most likable and trusted companion to the people.

But Fox hadn't forgotten about his plan. And soon he discovered where the people kept Sun when they weren't playing spear games with it. One day, Fox even spoke with Sun.

"Why do you let people pick on you like that?" asked Fox.

"What choice do I have?" Sun replied sadly. "I have no legs. It's not like I can just pick up and run away."

"Well, soon your troubles will be over," said Fox mysteriously. But he refused to say more.

Not long after this conversation, Sun was rolled out for a game. Fox—who had become a very skillful player—was invited to join in.

When it came his turn to roll Sun, Fox **assumed** the ready position. He made as if he was going to hurl Sun as far as he could. But instead, he grabbed it with his paws and started running back toward the dark side of the world.

As you can imagine, Sun was hot! If it hadn't been for the calluses from his long journey, Fox could never have carried the shining **orb.** Sun was also heavy. But Fox knew what to do about that. With a gentle voice, he **complimented** the brilliant ball.

"Sun," he said, pronouncing the name just right. "You're far too majestic to play these silly games with spears. You should be carried high above everyone's heads like the great leader you are."

Of course, Sun was flattered by these words. So flattered, in fact, that he nearly floated along on Fox's back. This helped Fox, for he was able to gain more and more speed.

Of course, the Other Side people were horrified to see Sun being taken from them. They immediately set out in pursuit of Fox.

But Fox was in luck. The sun lighted the path, which allowed Fox to take some shortcuts. Soon, Fox had left the Other Side people far behind. Now they had to make their way in the dim light which remained. Soon they would find out what it was like to be in the dark.

Fox ran for his very life. For he was sure the Other Side people wouldn't give up the chase easily.

Now Deer was assigned to meet Fox at a special meadow. Even though Fox had been gone for a long time, Deer was there just as he had promised. And it was a good thing too, for Fox was nearly exhausted by the time he arrived.

With the last of his strength, Fox tossed Sun to Deer. Sun landed in Deer's antlers. There he rode comfortably as the graceful animal leaped over streams and valleys.

But soon Deer's jumps grew shorter and shorter. He began to stumble, and Sun **jostled** loose into the sky. But much to Deer's relief, Magpie was there waiting, right where she had promised to be. With a wild dive, Magpie swooped under Sun and flew away with him toward Saynday.

"This is fun," said Sun to his new carrier. "I could get used to flying over everyone's heads."

"It's great!" replied Magpie, panting. "That is, if you don't have to carry a hot ball of fire. Ouch!"

Meanwhile, the Other Side people had been left behind. They weren't used to moving around in the dark and had lost their way. They spent quite a while bumping into each other and stubbing their toes on hard rocks. At last, they gave up their chase and went home.

When Magpie saw Saynday, she turned Sun over to him with relief. Saynday welcomed Sun and threw him over his shoulder as if he were carrying food. Staggering a bit under the weight, he began the short **trek** home. Soon the other animals caught up with Saynday as he **sauntered** along, enjoying Sun's new warmth and light.

"Look at this!" said Deer. "I can see trails to follow. And over there—brush and thickets to protect me!"

"Of course, it will be harder for me to hide," noted Fox. "But I guess it's worth it."

For a time, Saynday and his friends gloried in the light that Sun brought. They couldn't get enough of the beautiful sights that constantly met their eyes. Then one day, Magpie spoke up.

"Might we have too much of this Sun?" she asked with a worried look on her face. "Trees and plants are growing very fast now. Trees grow taller, even while I'm sitting in them."

"I don't wish to complain, but I'm very thirsty these days," confessed Fox.

"It's just plain hot," grumbled Deer.

"Something must be done, to be sure," Saynday agreed thoughtfully. "Perhaps we can find a better place to keep Sun."

"We'd better do something soon," gasped Magpie. "I don't think we'll last long in this heat."

Saynday tried several solutions. First, he placed Sun in

his own lodge. But Sun constantly complained about feeling cooped up. And Saynday—besides nearly sweating to death—kept bumping into the great ball of fire and burning himself.

"This will never work," said Saynday. He tried placing Sun on the roof of his lodge. But the heat began to burn a hole in it.

"My beautiful house!" cried Saynday. Then he lost his temper and hurled Sun into the sky as far as he could.

And there it stayed.

"That's better," said Fox.

"I hope it stays there," said Deer.

"Not too far, not too close," said Magpie. "Not too hot, and not too cold. Not too much light either. The sky is just the right place for Sun."

"Of course," said Saynday, pretending this was his idea all along. "I knew this would be the best solution! Sun will stay up in the sky. He can travel to the Other Side people and watch over them. Then he can travel back to watch over us. No spears or quarrelsome creatures can reach him there."

"And things will grow at just the right pace," said Magpie, Fox, and Deer in chorus.

So Saynday's plan for Sun worked out just right for all concerned. Sun must agree. For he's still up there in the sky, traveling from one side of the world to the other, giving light to all.

# INSIGHTS

According to Kiowa legend, their ancestors came into the world out of a cottonwood log. The people continued climbing from the log until a pregnant woman got stuck and blocked the way. According to the Kiowa, this is why their population is so low.

The early Kiowa settled in the mountains of western Montana. They remained there until a fight broke out over an antelope.

It happened when an antelope was killed. Two Kiowa chiefs disagreed over how to divide the animal. The disagreement grew into a bitter quarrel. As a result, the chief who lost took his group and headed northwest. The other group moved southeast, finally coming to the plains of western Kansas and eastern Colorado.

The Kiowa who went north were never heard from again. It may be that their group was too small to survive enemy attacks. However, there were a few rumors of a people living in the north who spoke a language like the Kiowa. For a long time, the Kiowa of the plains believed their relatives were still somewhere north of Montana.

According to Kiowa tradition, the greatest of the gods is the sun. In the time before European influence, the Kiowa held a yearly Sun Dance. The Sun Dance was performed to cure the illnesses of the tribe and to pray for gifts.

The last Kiowa Sun Dance was held in the late 1800s. There are two reasons it ended. First, part of the ritual was to kill a buffalo before the dance began. When buffalo got scarce, dances were canceled.

Even with a buffalo, though, sometimes dances couldn't be held for another reason—the white settlers.

They felt the dances were "uncivilized." Whenever the United States government heard that another dance was to occur, troops were sent to prevent it.

The Kiowa had war societies whose members gained honor by showing bravery in battle or other exploits. Members of these societies often went on raids for horses. Sometimes they would declare war on an enemy for the glory of it. And sometimes they fought for revenge.

Before fighting, Kiowa warriors often went off alone and fasted for several days, praying to the Great Spirit for courage.

Like many other peoples, the Kiowa buried their dead along with the dead person's property. After death, the person's name was never mentioned again. For a person's name was considered personal property. It was believed to be buried along with the body.

The current Kiowa tribe numbers more than 7,000 members, the majority of which live near Carnegie, Oklahoma. The main event of the tribe is the Kiowa Gourd Clan festival.

# TWO FEATHERS AND TURKEY BOY

## VOCABULARY PREVIEW

Below is a list of words that appear in the story. Read the list and get to know the words before you read the story.

**bizarre**—unusual; odd
**cast**—color; shade
**deceive**—fool; trick
**devoured**—eaten; consumed
**exotic**—strange; unusual
**famished**—starved; hungry
**finale**—finish; closing
**foretold**—predicted
**impostor**—fake; deceiver
**invincible**—unable to be overcome; unconquerable
**misgivings**—distress; anxiety
**noble**—great; grand
**quest**—search
**sinister**—evil; harmful
**wry**—ironic; sly

### Main Characters

**Impostor**—a sorcerer
**Turkey Boy**—Two Feathers' younger brother
**Two Feathers**—Turkey Boy's older brother
**Uncle**—Two Feathers' and Turkey Boy's uncle

### The Scene

Action takes place in the land of the Seneca in the northeast.

# Two Feathers and Turkey Boy

*Becoming an adult is never easy. But for Two Feathers, it was especially hard. He had to face many tests and dangers. And if he failed, his people would die out. Here is the story of Two Feathers' heroic attempt to save his people.*

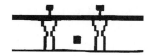

*L*ong ago, evil sorcerers had tremendous power in the world. They'd destroy whole families at a time. Out of one particular clan,[1] only three people survived—an old uncle and his two nephews. They lived all alone, far away from other people.

The uncle had known much better days and had done

---

[1] A clan is a group of related families.

many brave deeds. He was a keeper of the old ways—of sayings, stories, and powers. It was his duty to pass along his wisdom to his two nephews.

The younger of the two nephews was a small boy. He was about the size of a turkey gobbler. In fact, his robe was made of a turkey skin with all the feathers still on it. The little boy's arms fit into the turkey wings.

An odd outfit, you might say. But this turkey robe was not without magical powers. After all, it was made with the feathers of one of the finest birds around. So when the little brother put on his magic robe, he could fly up among the treetops. Because of this wonderful robe, he was called Turkey Boy.

The older of the two nephews was called Two Feathers. He was a responsible youngster, almost grown. And this is the story of his coming to manhood.

One day, Uncle realized that the time had come for Two Feathers to become an adult. Once Two Feathers became a man, he would have to find a wife. This was especially important now that the clan was so close to dying out.

"My nephew," said Uncle, "the day is at hand. It is customary for a youth of your age to leave his home and seek out his protective powers. Once found, these powers will help you throughout your life."

Two Feathers listened with great interest as Uncle told him what he had to do.

"Go to the river," instructed Uncle. "There you must fast[2] and wait for your protector. If you are patient, an animal will find you and share its power with you. Your brother will remain with me, for he is not yet old enough for this **quest.**"

Two Feathers followed Uncle's directions. He went to the river and built a small sweat lodge.[3] Then he sat down

---

[2] To fast means to go without food, sometimes for religious or spiritual purposes.

[3] A sweat lodge is a small hut heated by hot bricks. Many Native Americans use the sweat lodge to purify themselves and to seek visions.

and waited.

The young man fasted in the sweat lodge for many days. Each day he looked for the animal visitors who would share their power with him. But for nine days, none came. Still, Two Feathers did what he had been told to do. He fasted and waited longer still.

On the tenth day, Two Feathers was very weak from fasting. In fact, he was so **famished** he couldn't tell if he was awake or dreaming. Then a large spider dropped down on a great, twisted rope. In a raspy voice, the spider spoke to Two Feathers.

"I am Great Spider, and I am your protector," the creature said. "When you need help, call for me. I will assist you, my brother."

After these few words, Great Spider climbed up his spider rope and disappeared. Two Feathers was happy to have an ancient and wise protector like Great Spider.

But no sooner had Great Spider departed than another visitor came to Two Feathers. This time a black snake slithered out of a hole in the ground at Two Feathers' feet.

"Greetings, Two Feathers," hissed the snake. "I am Black Snake, your protector. Call for me whenever you need help."

Saying nothing more, Black Snake crawled back into the hole and disappeared. Two Feathers was once again alone in the sweat lodge. But despite his weakness from fasting, he felt new power come over him. He felt like a man. And he felt honored to have *two* protectors—not just one.

When Two Feathers returned home, Uncle immediately recognized the change in him. He rejoiced in his nephew's success. But Uncle was a little sad as well. For he knew that the young man would have to leave soon on a dangerous journey.

"Two Feathers, a man must have a wife," said Uncle. "You need a woman just as a woman needs a man. And a woman is needed here at our lodge. Women bring the promise of the future, for without them, our clan will die out."

Two Feathers listened carefully and nodded. Turkey Boy was listening, too, as Uncle continued.

"When I was young, I found a wife in a village close by," said Uncle. "But bad times have come. Sorcerers have driven the people of that village away. You must travel far to the east to find a companion. So prepare yourself well."

"I am shielded by my two animal protectors," said Two Feathers. "What more preparation do I need?"

Without a word, Uncle led Two Feathers to a bundle tied up in animal hides. The two nephews had never seen what was in that bundle, though they had often wondered about it.

"You will need more protection, my nephew," said Uncle. "Remove your clothes."

As Two Feathers did so, Uncle unrolled the bundle and took out a fine robe made of raccoon fur. Two Feathers draped the robe over his shoulders and stood before Uncle. The young man felt **noble** in this handsome garment.

"Not good enough," said Uncle with a shake of his head. "Take it off."

Uncle turned again to his secret bundle and took out a long shirt made of bobcat skins. It was even more impressive than the raccoon robe. The hair was short and bristled. The ears were sewn around the neck, and bobcat eyes were attached to the sleeves.

"My nephew," said Uncle, "this shirt allows anyone who wears it to see and to hear even while sleeping. Try it on and let me see how you look in it."

Two Feathers did as Uncle asked. It was a fine shirt, and one which Two Feathers liked very much. But Uncle still wasn't satisfied.

"You have a very difficult road ahead of you," said Uncle. "You'll need an even more powerful suit of clothes."

"What could be more powerful than this bobcat shirt?" asked Two Feathers as he pulled the garment off.

Uncle smiled. He dug down to the very bottom of the bundle. He pulled out something wrapped in soft doeskin. Uncle carefully opened the wrapping and revealed a shirt made of panther skin. Connected to the shirt was a cap made of a panther head. And the cap was adorned with two blue heron[4] feathers.

"Try this on," said Uncle, with satisfaction in his eyes. "This shirt is not just handsome, Nephew. The two heron feathers will watch out for you. And if you are in danger, they'll speak a warning."

Then Uncle reached into the bundle again. He handed Two Feathers a pouch made of a fisher skin,[5] an **exotic**-looking pipe, and a pair of sturdy moccasins. Then he gave Two Feathers a marvelous bow, complete with a full quiver of long-shafted arrows.

"The fisher-skin pouch is a living thing," said Uncle. "It will bite anyone who wishes to harm you."

Then Uncle pulled some roots out of the pouch. "This is medicine root," said Uncle. "Chew a small piece of it and you will be able to spit out wampum."[6]

"As you can see," continued Uncle, picking up the pipe, "the design on this pipe is of a bear accompanied by snakes. If an enemy bothers you, the bear will growl and the snakes will hiss. I would keep this pipe in the pouch as well.

"As for the bow and the long arrows," said Uncle gravely, "they are very powerful and accurate. However, only you will be able to use them."

"What about these moccasins?" asked Two Feathers.

"These, too, have magic power," explained Uncle. "You will be able to walk a great distance in a very short time with those moccasins on your feet."

---

[4] A heron is a long-necked water bird.
[5] A fisher is a large, dark brown animal related to the weasel.
[6] Wampum beads are made of polished shells strung onto belts. The beads were used as money by northeastern tribes.

Two Feathers was overcome with wonder. Now he had more help than just his animal protectors, Great Spider and Black Snake. He also had magical clothes and powerful weapons. In fact, he felt **invincible.** He felt that he had truly become a man.

"I am honored to accept these things, Uncle," said Two Feathers. "Surely I'm ready to begin my journey."

"Not yet," said Uncle. "There are other things you need to know. You must watch out and guard against certain dangers. Listen carefully, for your life depends on it. On your journey, you will come to three enchanted places. Any one of them can cause you great harm.

"First, you will come to a boy playing under an old oak tree," continued Uncle. "The boy will ask you to help him climb the tree and swing from it. Don't! For he is a witch's servant. And if this boy gets hold of you, he will carry you to the witch's lodge and drop you through the smoke hole. Then you'll be **devoured!"**

"I see," replied Two Feathers.

"Next on your journey," cautioned Uncle, "you will pass a deep spring of sparkling water. You will be thirsty, and the water will look inviting. But don't drink from it! Monsters dwell in that spring, and they'll pull you down into the water."

"No monsters for me," said Two Feathers. "I hear you clearly."

"And even farther along the trail," continued Uncle, "a **bizarre** old man will approach you, hopping on one foot. This man will be the most **sinister** threat to your safety. He will plead for help and ask you to shoot a raccoon for him. Whatever you do, don't listen to him. This old man is very dangerous. Do you understand all of these things, Nephew?"

"Yes, I think so, Uncle," replied Two Feathers. He repeated the tests he would have to face. "Tree and a boy. Spring and monsters. Old man and raccoon. I have it."

"Once you pass this last danger," continued Uncle, "you will be very near a village. There you will be able to find a bride."

Now, Turkey Boy had watched his brother's initiation[7] with some **misgivings.** Naturally, he felt left out of all the excitement. And he didn't like the thought of his brother's leaving. So he stepped forward and spoke his feelings.

"I'm not as old as Two Feathers," said Turkey Boy. "But I'm old enough to go with him on his journey."

"But who will stay here with me?" asked Uncle. "I'm old, and I will be lonely."

"But, Uncle," responded Turkey Boy, "I wouldn't know what to do here without Two Feathers. And he may need my help. Remember, I can fly. And I can give the cry of the wild turkey."

Uncle thought for a while. "I suppose you're right," he agreed at last. "Besides, two might be better than one on such a long and difficult road."

So after the final preparations were made, the two brothers set off in the search of a bride for Two Feathers. Turkey Boy flew on ahead and scouted out the turns and twists of the trail. He pointed out the way to his older brother.

Two Feathers took big strides in his magic moccasins. By noon, the brothers had gone as far as it would take an ordinary person three years to travel.

As Uncle **foretold,** the brothers came upon an old oak tree. And sure enough, playing under it was a small boy.

"Hey, travelers, I need to climb this tree," shouted the boy when he saw the brothers approach. "Would you give me a boost?"

Turkey Boy gave a warning cry that sounded like the call of a wild turkey. Two Feathers remembered Uncle's words. So instead of helping the boy, Two Feathers placed the boy on a stump beside the tree.

Immediately there was a tremendous roar. The stump—along with the boy—shot up into the sky and then dove down into the smoke hole of a witch's lodge

---

[7] An initiation is a ceremony in which a person (often a youth) is accepted as an adult member of a society.

some distance away.

"Our uncle was right," said Two Feathers. "It's a good thing Uncle warned us. Otherwise, I probably would have helped that boy."

"And you'd be a meal for a witch by now," added Turkey Boy.

"Well, that's the first test," sighed Two Feathers. "We have two more to go. Keep your eyes open."

The brothers traveled on. And before too long, they came upon the spring that Uncle had described.

Again, Turkey Boy gave a warning cry. And again, Two Feathers remembered what his uncle had told him. "This is no place to refresh my thirst," said Two Feathers to himself. "But perhaps I can make it safe for others to drink from later."

Pretending to take a drink, Two Feathers leaned over the edge of the spring. But he was very careful so as not to lose his balance. Suddenly a grotesque hand reached out of the spring and clawed at him.

"Aha!" shouted Two Feathers. "Uncle was right again."

The monster tried hard to pull Two Feathers in the water. But the young warrior was ready. He jerked the monster out of the spring and threw it on the ground.

"Guard this demon, Turkey Boy," said Two Feathers. "I'll see if there are any more of its kind in the water."

Turkey Boy stood guard over the monster while Two Feathers returned to the spring. Again, he leaned over very carefully. This time he was attacked by an even uglier creature. But he grabbed that demon by its muddy hair and flipped it into the clearing as well.

"Here's a friend for the first one, Brother," said Two Feathers. "See that they don't cause any mischief."

Then Two Feathers turned back to the spring for a third time. This time no monster attacked him, so he was able to drink. He took Turkey Boy a cool drink of the clear water.

Once the brothers drank the water, the spell that had

poisoned the spring was broken. With a shriek, the two monsters vanished into thin air.

A little farther along the path, the brothers approached a group of very tall trees. And just as Uncle had predicted, an old man was hopping about on one leg. He was doing a kind of dance and singing out, "Hai', hai', hai' hey, ya, hey. . . ."

When he saw the two brothers, he hopped over to them.

"You must rescue my raccoon," said the old man. "He's high up on that branch. If you can't rescue him, just shoot him for me so I can have his hide."

Turkey Boy, who was flying overhead, recognized the situation for what it was. He gobbled loudly and flapped his wings to warn Two Feathers.

But this old man reminded Two Feathers of his uncle. So Two Feathers immediately wanted to help the old man in any way he could. Undoubtedly some sorcery was at work, because this time Two Feathers forgot Uncle's warning.

In his eagerness to help the hopping man, Two Feathers quickly drew his bow and let fly an arrow. The arrow flew straight toward the raccoon's heart. But the raccoon was an illusion created by the old man. In a twinkle, the animal disappeared into a hole in the tree.

"But look here!" cried the old man. "You've let him get away! Well, this won't do! You must find him for me. I'm too old to climb up there, and I must have the hide."

"I'll climb up there for you," offered Two Feathers. "You remind me of my uncle, and I would do as much for him."

"But young man," said the old man slyly. "You wouldn't want to ruin that nice panther shirt and your other fine clothes. That tree is filthy. Why don't you take off your clothes and leave them with me? I'll guard them."

At this, the two feathers on the panther cap rattled together, making a warning sound. Turkey Boy was still flying overhead, flapping his wings and gobbling desperately. But Two Feathers paid no attention to either of them.

"You're right," Two Feathers said to the old man. "Uncle would want me to protect these clothes."

So, over Turkey Boy's loud protests, Two Feathers removed his magic shirt and the other items Uncle had given him. Then he climbed the tree and crawled to the hole where the raccoon had disappeared. Suddenly, Two Feathers heard a hideous laugh behind him. Through evil magic, the old man had flown up to the branch that Two Feathers stood on.

"Aha! foolish boy," cackled the old man. "You've forgotten your uncle's advice, haven't you? Well, it's too late now. I'm the keeper of this tree. And you'll find out soon enough what *that* means!"

With these words, the sorcerer shoved Two Feathers into the hole. The forgetful nephew tumbled headlong into the dark heart of the tree. He fell a long, long way before hitting the ground with a painful thud. Then with a deep groan, he fainted.

With Two Feathers out of the way, the old man flew to the ground. Then he picked up the fine panther shirt which Two Feathers had removed.

"Well, well, well," said the old man with an evil smirk. "This is my lucky day. This shirt has tremendous power. And so do these moccasins."

Then he looked at the bow and arrows. Unlike the clothes, they looked old and useless. So he left them on the ground.

Quickly the old man put on the clothes Two Feathers had left with him—the leggings, the pouch, and the panther shirt. And as soon as he was dressed, the old man looked like a strong young man. He looked just like Two Feathers. But he was a fraud, a pretender, an **impostor!**

"Now the magical protective power of these clothes is mine!" shouted Impostor to no one in particular. "I shall cross the river and claim myself a wife. She will see the image of a young man—not my shriveled and aged face."

With these words, Impostor walked away from the tree. And with each step, he looked more and more like a handsome young man. He left the bow and arrows lying there in the forest.

At first, Turkey Boy flew after the sorcerer, gobbling frantically. Then he thought to himself, "I can't leave Two Feathers all alone. I must stay and try to help him!" So he left Impostor and flew back to the evil tree.

Meanwhile, Impostor reached the river and swam across. At the other side, he met two sisters. The elder sister was attracted by his handsome face. She had no trouble believing his lies about being a fearless hunter. Indeed, she eagerly accepted his proposal of marriage. She proudly introduced Impostor to her father, the chief of the people on the river's other side.

"You seem like a fine young man," said Chief. "You have my approval to marry my daughter, if such is her wish."

So that very night, Impostor and the young woman were married and ate of the wedding bread.

Back at the tree, Two Feathers was just beginning to wake up. He looked around and saw that he had landed in a terrible place—a grave! All around him were the rotting remains of the old man's victims.

"The old man was a sorcerer!" said Two Feathers. "And he feeds on the remains of the dead! Why didn't I listen to Turkey Boy? He warned me to avoid that old man. Now the sorcerer has my magic clothes. Who knows what evil he is causing?"

Two Feathers called out for Turkey Boy. No answer came.

"No doubt that old man has eaten my brother as well," said Two Feathers in disgust and despair. "I'm doomed!"

Just then, Two Feathers remembered his protectors—Great Spider and Black Snake. If he ever needed help, it was now.

"Come, Great Spider! I need your help!" Two Feathers whispered.

Two Feathers leaned back and waited. He was far away from the place where he had first met Great Spider. He half-expected it to take a lifetime for his protector to come to him.

But suddenly a rope dropped down into the hole. Two Feathers grabbed it and felt himself being pulled up.

"Is that you, Turkey Boy?" Two Feathers asked.

"It is I, your protector, Great Spider," said a familiar voice. "Hold on. I will pull you up."

Once Two Feathers was out of the pit, he heard Great Spider's voice among the leaves and branches above his head. "Now I'll lower you to your freedom."

"How can I thank you?" asked Two Feathers as he was gently lowered to the ground.

"Just call on me when you need me," came the simple reply.

But suddenly, the spider's rope snapped.

"Help, Black Snake!" called Two Feathers. "I need *your* help now!"

And sure enough, Black Snake instantly appeared. His front end was wrapped around a branch. The rest of him was uncoiled and hanging down the tree. Two Feathers was able to cling to the snake's body and slide down to safety. Then the two protectors vanished as quickly as they had appeared.

All this time, Turkey Boy had been flying around overhead, desperately trying to think of something to do. Now he was thrilled to see his brother.

"I thought you were dead!" exclaimed Turkey Boy. "That sorcerer made off with your clothes. And now he looks just like you!"

"What shall we do?" asked Two Feathers. "I have no clothes, and I feel like an old man."

"Oof! And you smell like the dead," said Turkey Boy, backing away from his brother.

"I guess I've got no choice but to take the old man's

clothes and dress in them," said Two Feathers. "I just hope the young women can see past my outer appearance."

"And smell past your odor!" added Turkey Boy with a **wry** smile.

"Well, at least I still have my special bow and arrow," remarked Two Feathers, picking them up from where Impostor had left them.

The two brothers headed for the river and crossed it. On the other side, they met the younger sister of Impostor's new wife.

"I'm a young man in search of a wife," Two Feathers said to her. "Are you interested?"

The younger sister stared at Two Feathers.

"What have we here?" she asked. "You look like an old man to me. Didn't you say you were young? Do you **deceive** yourself so? Who are you, really?"

So Two Feathers told her everything that had happened. He told her about the terrible pit of bones, about the old man who was now pretending to be young. And he introduced her to Turkey Boy, who was flying nervously from tree to tree.

Younger Sister looked closely into Two Feathers' eyes. Then she said, "I believe you. I think some of the bones you found in that tree were my brothers' bones. For both of my brothers went out that way to hunt, and they never returned."

"And so you'll marry me?" asked Two Feathers.

"Yes," came Younger Sister's reply. "Since I need a husband, I will marry you. You have an air of truth about you, despite your poor appearance—and bad odor," she added, wrinkling her nose with distaste.

So Younger Sister—soon to be known as New Wife— took Two Feathers and Turkey Boy home. There she presented her husband-to-be to her father.

"I wish to marry this man," she said to her father. "He is honest and trustworthy."

Impostor was also in the lodge, and he immediately

recognized Two Feathers.

"Father-in-law," said Impostor, "I wouldn't trust this man. You know there are sorcerers in the land. He could be after your wealth."

"I'll make that decision," responded Chief to Impostor. "I have a great desire to see all my daughters married before I die. And Younger Sister seems to know her own mind. I therefore grant her wish. She has my blessing to marry this man."

Younger Sister then took Two Feathers into her lodge. She showed him her beautiful bed with its soft deerskin pillows. Herbs hung from the walls, and the wall coverings were decorated with beautiful porcupine quill designs.

"Turkey Boy can sleep up there," she said, pointing to a special loft.[8]

Few villagers had spoken to Two Feathers since his arrival in the village. They were disgusted by his appearance and horrible smell. Impostor, on the other hand, was popular because of his good looks. All the village women admired him.

But Impostor's improved looks hadn't changed his soul. He was such a coward at heart that he refused to go hunting. His wife was suspicious of this at first. After all, didn't he claim to be a great hunter? But she liked gazing at her husband so much that she overlooked his other failings.

Chief held a feast to celebrate the weddings of his two daughters. All the people gathered around Impostor and listened to every word he spoke. But poor Two Feathers was left alone.

Then it came time for the people to smoke a pipe together. Impostor reached in the fisher-skin pouch for the bear pipe. But as soon as he stuck his fingers in the pouch, the fisher bit him as hard as it could.

"Ouch!" Impostor yelled. He began dancing around

---

[8] A loft is a floored space under the roof of a house.

the lodge shaking his hand.

"What is it?" asked his wife.

"Nothing," lied Impostor. He certainly didn't want his new wife to suspect anything.

In the confusion, the fisher pouch dropped to the ground. Two Feathers picked it up without anyone else noticing. Sneaking a looking inside the pouch, he found that everything was still there, including the medicine root and the pipe.

"At least I have my pouch back," thought Two Feathers with relief. "Now it's just a matter of time. Impostor will soon be sorry he tricked me!"

That night, Two Feathers reached into the fisher pouch and took out the special root Uncle had given him. He asked New Wife to bring him a large bowl.

When the bowl came, Two Feathers chewed a piece of the magic root. Then he opened his mouth and blew into the bowl. To everyone's amazement, fine wampum was in the bowl. Two Feathers filled the bowl to the brim and then some.

"Take this gift to your father," said Two Feathers to New Wife. "He will approve, I am sure."

"I will do so immediately," said New Wife. She was amazed at her husband's marvelous ability.

"You've got one fine husband," said Chief to New Wife, upon seeing the bowl. "I've never seen such quality wampum. Hooray for him—and for us!"

Of course, Impostor heard of Two Feathers' gift. And he became wild with jealousy.

"Wife," called Impostor, "bring me a bowl. I'll show this upstart brother-in-law who gives the best gifts."

Immediately, Impostor began blowing into the bowl. But instead of producing wampum, he spit out an awful mixture of foul lizards and worms. For that was Impostor's diet when he couldn't eat human flesh.

"Take this bowl to your father," ordered Impostor. "No doubt he will be amazed by my abilities."

Chief was amazed, all right. He coughed and gagged.

"Get that foul stuff out of here!" Chief ordered angrily. "And tell that husband of yours to stay out of my lodge. This is disgusting!"

Now up until then, Impostor had always been careful not to take off Two Feathers' special clothes. He knew that his true identity would be revealed if he did. He even slept in those clothes.

But on that fateful night, Impostor had eaten too much. In fact, he was so stuffed that the clothes were too tight. So he foolishly took the clothes off and tossed them at the foot of the bed.

Impostor slept late the next morning, while Two Feathers was up bright and early to hunt with his magic bow. Two Feathers killed a great number of deer. In fact, he brought back enough game to last the entire year.

As he returned from the hunt, Two Feathers happened to spy his clothes through an opening in Impostor's lodge. Quietly he crept in and reclaimed them.

The clothes were tattered and torn. But as soon as Two Feathers put them on, they were restored to their original condition. Not only that, Two Feathers' appearance began to change. His color returned. His muscles toned up immediately. And his teeth lost their yellow **cast.** He looked marvelous.

Two Feathers went straight to the tribal council.[9] To demonstrate his powers, he pointed the magic pouch at a maiden, and she fell down dead. Then he whisked it the other direction, and she was restored to life. Next, Two Feathers lit his pipe. The bear rose and stretched and growled. The snakes on the stem wriggled and hissed as if alive.

Then the panther eyes on Two Feathers' cap blinked, and the heron feathers began to sing. They sang an ancient song from the dimness of the tribal memory. For a **finale,** Two Feathers made wampum before the council's wide and amazed eyes. Well, you can imagine what the

[9] Many tribes were governed by a group of elders known as a council.

council thought of this masterful display of talent and showmanship.

Of course, Impostor was powerless without the magic clothes. He slept on and on. And when his wife looked in at him, she now saw a wrinkled old man. She was disgusted by the sight and scolded the villain.

"How could you do this to me?" she yelled at Impostor. "You have humiliated me before my people!"

Then she scooped Impostor up like trash and took him to the village dump. There she tossed him into a mudhole. Turkey Boy soared on high, watching as Impostor sank to the very bottom and took his last gasp of air.

Later, the people gathered around Two Feathers and Turkey Boy.

"Long ago," Two Feathers said to Chief, "your people and mine were as one. But due to the work of the sorcerers, we were separated. And in the land where I come from, there are only my uncle, my brother, and myself left.

"As I traveled to this land, I met those evil sorcerers, and I disposed of every one of them," Two Feathers continued. "So now I would like to invite you and all your people back to my land—*our* land."

"I must consult the council," Chief replied. "But I think they will all agree that returning to our original homeland would be a wise move."

Chief was right. So the people prepared to make the trip back to the home of their ancestors. Of course, they did not all have magic moccasins or robes that could fly, so it was a long walk for them. But Two Feathers and Turkey Boy stayed with them every step of the way.

The journey took years and years. As they traveled along, Turkey Boy took off his feathered robe. He dressed in a warrior's fashion, with large silver bracelets and many strands of beads. And when the time came, he found a loving wife as well.

At long last, Two Feathers, Turkey Boy, their wives, and all of the people finally reached Uncle's lodge. Uncle was pleased beyond telling. He thanked his nephews and blessed all the new arrivals. And then he turned over his rule to Two Feathers and the new generations to come.

The story of Two Feathers and Turkey Boy shows that the quest for adulthood is sometimes long and hard. There are many tests along the way. But they are worth meeting, worth the attempt to prove our courage.

And we may think that we can overcome our tests alone. But Two Feathers' story shows that even heroes ask for help sometimes.

# INSIGHTS

**S**torytelling is an important part of Native American culture. Not only is it a form of entertainment. It is also a way of passing down the history and traditions of the people.

Storytellers themselves are valued members of the community. People listen carefully to the storyteller's tales. Afterwards, listeners often give the teller a small gift to show their appreciation.

"Two Feathers and Turkey Boy" is a popular story among the Seneca. But according to a storytelling tradition, it can only be told during the winter. As important as storytelling is, it is forbidden to tell certain stories during the summer.

"Little people," or wood fairies, are said to punish those who break the no-summer-storytelling law. A wood fairy might fly around in the form of a beetle or bird, looking for offenders. If the wood fairy finds a violator, it will make sure the chief knows.

If the offender continues, a bee might sting the storyteller's lips. Failing that, snakes might to choke the teller while sleeping. Various punishments will continue until the criminal storyteller stops.

Besides historical tales, the Seneca also enjoy ghost stories. One favorite has to do with a meat-eating skeleton who chases travelers at night and eats them. Other tales tell of evil stone giants or of a giant mosquito.

In the days before European influences, storytellers were entrusted with the entire history of their people. Sometimes, so much information was hard to remember.

*continued*

To help them remember, storytellers kept belts made of wampum beads. These beads were strung and woven into different designs which the storyteller was able to interpret.

Wampum was valued for other reasons as well. It was often used as money.

In the myth, Impostor was able to take on the look of Two Feathers. Transformation of this sort is common in Seneca stories.

Not only are people able to change themselves into animals or other people. They can also change into trees or rocks.

In the days before European influence, the Seneca lived in buildings made of bark called longhouses. Screens divided a longhouse into family apartments. Each of these apartments was equipped with its own fireplace and smokehole in the roof. A fairly large village might consist of several longhouses, each over 100 feet long. Today longhouses are used for special ceremonies and festivals.

# TRICKSTERS

## Coyote and the Thundering Rock
## The One Who Sets Things Right

Tricksters are characters found in myths from almost all cultures. These sly creatures often cause big trouble.

Native Americans tell stories about several different tricksters. Three of the most important are Coyote, Hare, and Raven. Each of these is something like the animal he's named after. But each has some human or superhuman qualities as well.

Native American trickster myths are often humorous. But they are not less important for that reason. Many Native American people see great wisdom in the antics of the trickster. For he teaches that life is full of creative possibilities. In fact, some myths honor the trickster as the creator himself.

# COYOTE AND THE THUNDERING ROCK

# VOCABULARY PREVIEW

Below is a list of words that appear in the story. Read the list and get to know the words before you read the story.

**absurd**—ridiculous; silly
**admirable**—good; worthy
**benevolent**—kindly; generous
**capacity**—ability
**careening**—rolling and swaying wildly
**consented**—agreed
**dread**—fear
**evasions**—dodges; attempts to escape
**flourish**—showy movement; display
**generosity**—giving
**negotiation**—discussion; finding middle ground
**pelt**—animal skin
**pray**—say; please (tell me)
**precious**—valuable
**unyielding**—stubborn; bullheaded

## Main Characters

**Coyote**—trickster
**Iktome**—Coyote's friend; also known as Spiderman
**Iya**—a rock

## The Scene

The action takes place on the great plains.

# Coyote

 **and the**

# Thundering Rock

*Playful and full of life—that's Coyote. But sometimes he gets a bit careless of others' feelings. Then things can get dangerous for Coyote. Keep that in mind if you ever find yourself traveling with him!*

**O**ne day Coyote was traveling along with his old friend and sidekick, Iktome.[1] They were talking about this and that when their path happened to take them by a special place—as paths sometimes do. What made this place special was a rock. Don't be surprised by that. Rocks can be unusual too.

This rock's name was Iya,[2] and it was different from other rocks. Any rock can absorb heat from the sun

[1] (ik tō´ mē)
[2] (ē´ ya)

during the day to keep it warm at night. And most rocks are solid and strong. Rocks can also resist the constant wear of Wind and Water and Time. But Iya's abilities went beyond those of ordinary rocks. Iya had real power, real medicine!

Now Coyote was good at noticing the **capacity** of others. He saw right away that the rock was special. But even Coyote had no way of knowing just how much medicine Iya really had. Coyote and Iktome both would learn soon enough.

"Look over here," Coyote said to Iktome, grinning and nodding like a wise old man. "Did you notice this rock? I bet you would have passed right by it if I hadn't mentioned it."

Iktome went over and looked at the rock. "Well, it's pretty in its own way," said Iktome.

"Pretty!" exclaimed Coyote. "Have you no eyes, Iktome? Can't you see that this is quite a special rock? Look at the shape and color. Notice the lines of green moss—they're like the lines of its life story. This rock deserves a gift. I just happen to have the perfect thing for it."

With a **flourish,** Coyote whirled off the blanket he was wearing and draped it over the rock.

"Wear this finely woven blanket in good health, **admirable** rock," said Coyote. "It will keep you from freezing and cracking on cold nights."

Iktome listened to Coyote's offer to the rock and was a bit surprised by his friend's **generosity.** He raised an eyebrow at Coyote.

"What a free-spirited gift, Coyote," said Iktome. "What puts you in such a generous mood today? And don't you have a gift for *me,* old friend that I am?"

"Don't be so jealous," responded Coyote, lifting his nose in the air. "To listen to you talk, one would think I never give anything away. You know that I'm a **benevolent** sort. Besides, I feel in harmony with the world today. And a royal rock such as this should be rewarded. My gift to you will come in due course."

What did come to both Iktome and Coyote was a cold rain shower. First, the skies turned dark with clouds. Then came rain which turned to hail. And then the hail turned to freezing drizzle, and the ground became slush.

"There's a cave up in that hill," said Iktome.

"Thank goodness for that!" replied Coyote.

"I bet you would have passed right by it if I hadn't mentioned it," added Iktome.

"Don't be silly," growled Coyote between shivers. "Of course I saw it. I was just going to suggest that we seek shelter there. I'm wet through and through."

Even the cave was cold and damp. Coyote grew colder and colder. The drizzle still fell outside.

"It sure would be nice to have my blanket back," said Coyote to himself. Then Coyote looked over at Iktome, who wore a warm buffalo robe.

"Say, good friend," said Coyote. "Would you do me a tiny little favor?"

"What's that?" asked Iktome.

"Would you go back down the slope and find that rock? You know, the one I gave my blanket to?"

"And?" asked Iktome with **dread** in his voice.

"Well, couldn't you just quietly remove my blanket and bring it back? After all, Iya started with no covering other than moss. Being just a rock, he'll never miss my blanket."

"Friend," said Iktome. "I'll go to Iya as you ask me. But I won't take his blanket without asking first. That would be stealing."

"Okay, okay," **consented** Coyote. "But hurry. I'm freezing."

It didn't take Iktome long to find Iya. And when he did, he placed his hand on the rock as if they were old friends.

"Sorry, Iya," said Iktome, "but I must ask you for this blanket. You see, Coyote has changed his mind. He's wet and cold and would like it back."

"What is given once is always given," said Iya coldly. "Besides, I've grown to enjoy my blanket. Away with you, Iktome."

Iktome sighed. He had expected this kind of answer. So he left the blanket on the rock and walked slowly back to the cave.

"Iya said to forget it," reported Iktome to Coyote. "Iya thinks the blanket is his—and he's right, you know."

"What!" shouted Coyote in alarm. "That ungrateful, hardheaded. . . " Angrily, Coyote kicked one of the rocks in the cave. It was just an ordinary rock, but it nearly broke Coyote's foot.

"Ooouch!" Coyote howled. "Rocks are ugly and hard and **unyielding.** That's why they have such bad reputations."

Coyote hopped around the cave holding his toe. "I'll go and get my blanket myself," he said. "And I'll give Iya a piece of my mind while I'm at it!"

"Think twice about this, friend," said Iktome. "Iya's no ordinary rock. You said so yourself. Just forget your blanket. Come. I'll share my robe."

"Don't be **absurd!**" steamed Coyote. "I know what I'm doing. That blanket is mine!"

So Coyote trotted back through the ice and slush to where Iya sat under the blanket.

"Rock, you have no need for my blanket," said Coyote. "If you needed a blanket, nature would have given you one. Do you see any other rocks wrapped in blankets? No, you don't. So give me my blanket immediately! This is beyond **negotiation!**"

"No, Coyote," replied Iya calmly. "You can chase your own tail for all I care. This is my blanket now. You gave it. I keep it. Enough said."

"I've heard that rocks are dumb," said Coyote. "Now I know. If you think I will stand here and catch cold and allow you to wear my warm blanket, you're deaf *and* dumb."

With these words, Coyote reached out and grabbed

the blanket and snatched it away from Iya.

"You'll regret this, Coyote," said the rock in a firm voice. "It is well to give. But to take back what has been given is foolish!"

But Coyote ignored Iya's words. He turned and walked back to the cave. There he warmed himself in the softness of his fine blanket. It still held some of Iya's heat.

Finally the sun came out again. And so did Coyote and Iktome. They stepped out into the sunshine, stretched, and ate some pemmican, fry-bread, and wojapi.[3]

After their delicious meal, they decided to have a smoke before they resumed their journey. Coyote was just lighting up his pipe when they were startled by a thundering noise.

**"Pray,** what's that sound?" asked Coyote, still holding his pipe.

"I don't know, but it seems to be getting closer."

"It sounds like thunder. But the storm is gone. I wonder what it could be?"

Then Iktome saw something coming from behind Coyote. He jumped up.

"Don't look back!" Iktome said. "Just *run!*"

"But why?" asked Coyote.

"You don't want to know," replied Iktome. "But if you don't run now, you'll lose your blanket again, to say nothing of your **precious** little life."

"What do you mean?" demanded Coyote.

"Get up, you fool! Here comes Iya!"

Coyote glanced back just in time to see Iya **careening** toward them. Coyote scrambled to his feet and started running as fast as he possibly could.

"The river! Head for the river, friend!" yelped Coyote.

"See what your *friendship* has gotten me," panted Iktome to Coyote as he ran along. "Do me a favor and don't call me 'friend' at times like this!"

---

[3] (pem´ i cən) Pemmican is dried meat and berries. Fry-bread is quick bread made by deep-fat frying. (wu ja´ pē) Wojapi is soup made of berries.

"Quit your complaining!" said Coyote. "We'll be safe in the river. Rocks can't swim. They can't even float."

The frightened pair swam across the river as fast as they could. But such **evasions** meant nothing to the rock. Iya simply skipped straight over the river as if it weren't there.

"Run into the forest," called Coyote, looking over his shoulder. "Surely this rock won't be able to roll among the big trees."

This time, Iktome said nothing. But he did follow Coyote into the forest.

But Iya just kept rolling on. He crashed and thundered through the tall pines and splintered them into tiny pieces. This rock was determined!

Indeed, the rock chased Coyote and Iktome all the way back to the flatlands. The two were breathing hard now.

"Look, Coyote," said Iktome between huffs and puffs, "this whole affair really isn't my concern. Besides, I have another appointment to keep. So, see you later."

Before Coyote could blink an eye, his companion turned into a spider and disappeared into a mouse hole.

Coyote was on his own. He took one look over his shoulder and kicked into his fastest gallop. His feet were a whir of motion, barely skimming the top of the ground. He had never run this fast, not even in pursuit of the swiftest rabbit.

But when Coyote glanced back over his shoulder, he howled with fear. The rock was gaining on him! Just three steps later, Iya caught up with Coyote. With a thunderous roar, Iya rolled right on over the madly running Coyote. The rock squashed Coyote flat!

"How do you like your flat face now, blanket giver?" taunted Iya. "Try to howl now."

And, adding insult to injury, Iya jerked the blanket away from the flattened Coyote. Then the rock carried the blanket back to his own special place.

Shortly after Iya left, a rancher came riding by. He

noticed Coyote sprawled out on the prairie.

"What a nice rug," said the rancher. "I think I'll take this home."

The rancher reached down from his horse and picked up Coyote's scruffy form. He took the **pelt** home to decorate his floor.

Don't worry about Coyote, though. You know how tough he is. "Never say die" is his motto. Even so, he couldn't just get up and walk away. Coyote was still as flat as a rug.

That night, Coyote managed to draw in enough breath to puff himself up a little bit. Then he held his breath and breathed in some more. All night he pumped air back into his lungs. Finally he got back to his normal shape. By sunrise, Coyote was able to get up and run away.

That morning, the rancher's wife was surprised to discover that her new rug was gone. She woke her husband to show him. When they looked out the front door, they saw coyote footprints leading away from the house.

"I guess our rug ran away," said the rancher's wife, with a sigh. "Next time, be sure you get a dead one."

Coyote has been running ever since. And he still looks over his shoulder. He never knows when an angry rock might come thundering over him. And if you could run alongside Coyote, he'd make this wise suggestion:

"When you feel generous of heart, be sure that you're sincere."

Maybe someday he'll follow his own advice.

Don't count on it, though.

# INSIGHTS

**T**ales about tricksters have been popular since storytelling began. In Native American lore of the plains, Coyote is the great trickster. In the east, the trickster is Hare. In the northwest, Raven sometimes acts the part.

The trickster often seems like a clown. He deliberately breaks rules, and at times, he is blamed for bringing great evil to the world. Oddly enough, the trickster is honored by many people. Perhaps he represents the unexpected in life.

In traditional Sioux culture, living arrangements were governed by taboos. Certain people were forbidden to speak to certain other members of a family.

For example, a young married couple might live for a short time with one or the other's parents. But this was an uneasy situation. For a wife was forbidden to look at or speak to her father-in-law. And a husband couldn't look at or address his mother-in-law. Small wonder the young couple was quickly given their own tipi!

A Sioux's blood family was very important—even more important than a spouse. One was more likely to perform a generous deed for a brother or sister than for a husband or wife.

In Sioux culture, grandparents are held in great respect. And they play a great role in child-rearing. The term "grandparent" is sometimes used when referring to supernatural beings. For example, prayers to *Wankan Tanka*—the Great Spirit—might start, "Grandfather, Great Spirit."

One of the most important objects in the ceremonial life of the Sioux is the sacred pipe. The "Grand Pipe," as it is called, is about three feet long and is painted with sacred symbols. It is believed that the smoke of the pipe carries prayers to all parts of the universe.

According to legend, the sacred pipe was brought to the Sioux by White Buffalo Woman.

White Buffalo Woman appeared from the west as a beautiful woman. She gave the people the pipe and showed them the proper way to use it. In the process, she taught the people the proper way to live and pray.

Then the woman walked away in the direction from which she had come. But before she disappeared, she rolled over four times. Each time, she appeared as a buffalo of a different color. The last time she rolled over, she appeared as a white buffalo. According to the Sioux, the white buffalo is the most sacred of all creatures.

# THE ONE WHO SETS THINGS RIGHT

## VOCABULARY PREVIEW

Below is a list of words that appear in the story. Read the list and get to know the words before you read the story.

**coaxed**—persuaded; helped
**complacent**—self-satisfied; smug
**confront**—challenge; stand up to
**distraught**—upset; disturbed
**doting**—adoring; pampering
**incantation**—spell
**indignantly**—angrily
**persistent**—continuous; constant
**privilege**—special right
**pulsating**—beating; throbbing
**ravenous**—greedy; eager for food
**recede**—go back; withdraw
**scoundrel**—bad person; rascal
**sulking**—pouting
**unrelenting**—determined; not giving in

## Main Characters

**Daughter**—Old One's daughter; mother of Raven
**Old One**—source of all things
**Raven**—trickster

## The Scene

The action takes place after the creation of people, but before the sun, moon, and stars were revealed.

# The One Who Sets Things Right

*Raven is known as the One Who Sets Things Right. Oh, sometimes he forgets important things. Leaving a world in darkness does present a bit of a problem. But whenever Raven makes mistakes, he always tries to make things better. You can count on it.*

**H**e's very generous, that Raven. He gave many things to the people of the earth. To start with, he made rivers. Then he filled them with different kinds of fish—big and small fish, fast and slow fish. Raven also scattered the seeds for fruit trees and vines all across the land. Before long, the whole world was filled with food that Raven had provided for people to eat.

But Raven had overlooked one small detail. He'd forgotten all about light. There was no Sun, nor Moon, nor even stars.

Not that people missed light particularly, never having seen or heard of it. They were used to making their way through the dark. You see, sound was very important to them. They found rivers by listening for the rushing of water. And they caught fish by listening for their jumping sound.

But Raven realized that things could be better. He knew that it was hard living in the dark, trying to catch fish with no light. So he paid his human friends a visit.

"Hello, my friends," said Raven. "It's me, Raven. I'm the dark-feathered fellow who is as dark as the darkness that surrounds you."

"Why, Raven!" said the people, groping about in the dark. "How kind of you to pay us a visit! Not to seem rude, but we're very busy trying to catch fish, and we don't have much time for talk. So what's your business?"

"Well, you probably know my nickname," explained Raven. "The One Who Sets Things Right. And that's exactly why I'm here. This world I've made for you could be made just a tad bit better."

"But how?" asked the people. "We're very grateful to you for the fish in the rivers and the fruits on the land. What more could we ask?"

"I know where I can find you some light," offered Raven.

"Light?" asked the people. "What's that?"

"It would take too long to explain," responded Raven. "But trust me. You'll like it. And it'll make your lives much easier."

"Whatever you say," said the people. "But it does seem a pity for you to trouble yourself. Creation is pretty nearly perfect, as far as we're concerned."

And they went back to fishing in the dark.

Now what Raven had said was true. He knew that Sun and Moon and the stars lived up the world's largest river in the house of the Old One. That place was known as the Source of All Things. Raven himself had been created there, long, long ago. Somehow, he had to go back to the Source and get Sun and Moon and the stars. But how was he to do it?

"It'll take a trick or two," said Raven to himself. "But I've got a whole bag of tricks. They don't call me the One Who Sets Things Right for nothing. Ah, I believe I have a plan!"

And in an instant, Raven disappeared. You see, he had turned himself into an unborn baby. And not just *any* unborn baby. He was to be the son of the Old One's daughter, who lived at the Source of All Things. So Raven was reborn as a baby in the Old One's house.

It was soon clear that the Old One's grandchild was no ordinary baby. The day after he was born, Raven stood up in his basket. The day after that, he crawled. The day after that, he walked. And the day after that, he talked— or at least he made sounds.

"Ga, ga, ga!" cried Raven. Or as a raven might normally put it, "Caw, caw, caw!" Did you ever notice that babies and ravens speak the same language? Now you know why.

Now the Old One was—well, very old. And naturally, he was a **doting** and proud grandparent. So when he heard his new grandchild talk so early in life, he bragged to everyone about it.

"Just look at those eyes!" he exclaimed. "Why, they're as sharp and observant as a raven's!"

Little did he know!

Well, everyone was delighted by the new child. But one thing bothered the baby's mother and grandfather. The baby wouldn't eat. They didn't know that the baby was really Raven, who had no need for food.

The baby refused deer fat, mutton fat, and even tallow.[1] He would chew on a piece of fat, but then he would

---

[1] Tallow is a hard kind of fat used in making candles and soap.

spit it out. The Old One and his daughter were afraid the baby would starve without any food. So the baby's mother tried a trick of her own.

The mother took a piece of a fish called the bullhead and wrapped it in a big piece of fat. Now bullhead is a particularly good-tasting fish. So she knew that once the baby tasted it, he would surely want more.

And she was right. The baby chewed on the big piece of fat until he reached a shred of bullhead. He liked the flavor and swallowed the piece of fish. Right away, he cried out for more.

"You're finally hungry!" said the mother. "Now you won't starve! You'll live for sure!"

But no sooner had the baby eaten than he was hungry again. So his mother fed him again. The baby ate, and then he cried again. And so began a long train of meals that lasted, one right after the other, for several days.

In fact, the baby ate so much that the Old One grew worried. "This child is a bottomless pit!" complained the Old One. "Will he never stop eating? We're going to run out of all the food we've got stored up!"

So the Old One's family had traded one problem for another. Now the baby was either eating or crying all the time.

Well, this was all part of Raven's plan. For when he cried, he tilted his head back and looked up into the rafters of the house. His eyes searched for some sign of Sun or Moon or the stars. Eventually he saw what he was looking for—three very large bags hanging high in the rafters.

He studied the bags with those sharp eyes. He figured that the one on the left held the sun, for it glowed brightly. And he figured that the one on the right held the moon, for it glowed more softly. And he assumed that the middle bag held the stars, for it twinkled.

"Oh, this is almost too easy!" Raven said to himself. "This business of pretending to be a baby is my best trick yet. Still, I'm not through this yet. The rest of the job will take patience as well as craftiness."

"Ga! Ga! Ga! Ga! Ga!" Raven cried again and again, pointing at the bags in the rafters. The baby's mother tried everything she could think of to stop the crying. She rocked the baby, sang to him, talked baby talk with him. But nothing would get the baby to stop. He just kept pointing at those bags in the rafters, as if he wanted them for toys.

You know how that can get on your nerves. Even if you love a little baby, that kind of crying, crying, crying can really get to you after a while.

"Listen, Father," the mother said to the Old One one day. "Couldn't Baby play with just one of those big bags up there? Just one? Perhaps the twinkling one? Please? I've tried everything else."

"No!" replied the Old One with alarm. "Heavens, no! How could you even suggest it? Those bags have special medicine. You should know that. You were never allowed to play with them when you were little. Why should this grandchild have that **privilege?"**

But the baby kept crying. And a grandfather's heart is even softer than a parent's heart. So finally, Old One climbed a ladder to the rafters and brought down the bag that twinkled.

"Here," said the Old One to his daughter. "Let him play with this. But whatever you do, don't let him open the bag."

The daughter handed the bag to Baby, and he immediately stopped crying.

"See there!" she said with a sigh of relief. "That's all he wanted!"

Then the Old One and his daughter went away to take well-deserved naps. Raven's plan was working. He squeezed the bag and sat watching the twinkling lights shining through its sides. Then he pulled the bag's drawstring.

*Whooosh!*

Just like magic, the stars streamed up through the

smoke hole in the ceiling and scattered into a million different places into the sky. Some of the stars formed special outlines which we recognize even today.

The noise of the escaping stars woke the Old One and his daughter immediately. And of course, the Old One was very angry.

"He's let one of my treasures escape!" cried the Old One. "What kind of child do you have here, Daughter? He's surely no grandson of mine!"

But even the Old One couldn't get the stars back now. All he could do was try to keep Raven quiet.

But remember the bullhead? Raven was still hungry all the time—as he is to this day. His appetite was—how shall we say it?—**ravenous.** So the grandfather and his daughter kept giving Raven more food. All kinds of food. He liked to eat anything and everything—and did.

Not only was Raven's plan working, but he was getting fed on top of it! Raven was pretty pleased with himself. But he couldn't grow **complacent.** His task was not yet finished.

Raven kept up the eating—and the crying. He cried so hard and kept pointing to the rafters that finally Old One could stand it no longer.

"I don't believe this younger generation," said Old One as he climbed to the rafters again. "There's no pleasing them."

Old One took down the second bag, the one that glowed more softly. He handed it to Raven with a special request.

"Keep it tied this time, you bawling baby. Allow me some peace and quiet in my old age."

Raven followed the same routine. He stopped crying and pretended to play with the bag. And when no one was looking, he untied the drawstring.

*Whisk,* the glowing disk of the moon sailed right through the smoke hole in pursuit of the stars.

"What?" cried the Old One. "You've let my second treasure escape? What kind of child do you have here,

Daughter? He seems like no real relative of mine."

But Raven was **unrelenting.** He kept up his crying.

"Ga! Ga! Ga! Ga! Ga! Ga! Ga! Ga!"

It truly drove the Old One out of his wits. Finally he could stand it no longer. He hobbled up the ladder again and ripped down the brightest bag. Then he secured the string with a double knot.

"You're a spoiled child!" he growled down from the rafters. "I'll give you this bag if you'll only stop your crying. My old ears can't stand much more!"

Then he threw the bag at the baby, almost hitting the child on its head.

"Father, be careful!" scolded Daughter. "You almost knocked my poor baby unconscious!"

Now the knot the Old One had tied would be far too hard for you or me to untie. But we know Raven by now, don't we? Not even a double knot could stop him for long.

But even for him, this was a particularly nasty knot. He tried again and again to untie it, but it remained secure. No matter, though. The baby just cried out "Ga! Ga!" and turned back into the form of Raven.

The Old One and his daughter couldn't believe their eyes. Raven flew through the smoke hole with the shiny Sun bag dangling from his beak. The reflections of the sun's rays glistened on Raven's feathers. It was a pretty sight, most people would agree.

Raven flew down the Source River until he spotted people fishing on the bank. It was a clear night and brighter than anything they had seen before. They were using Moon's light to cast their nets and lines in just the right places.

As we know, Raven had developed a real hunger for food. After all, he had got a taste of that bullhead fish and couldn't get enough of it.

"Give me something to eat, people," cawed Raven. "I'm the One Who Sets Things Right, remember?"

Now we know that some people don't always think of

others. And that was the case with these particular folks. They were ungrateful, forgetting how much Raven had helped them so far. They didn't even bother to thank him for the precious Moon.

"Catch your own fish, black-winged one," they snapped back. "And stop your cawing! You'll scare the fish!"

"Well!" replied Raven **indignantly,** flying farther down the river. "I'll just find a more grateful clan!"[2]

So Raven flew on until he came to another group of people. There he asked again for the favor of food.

"Caw! Caw! Caw!" called the bird. "I'm Raven, the hungry one, the starving one. Please give me some fish. In return, I will give you Sun, which I carry in this bag. You'll have more light than ever by which to fish."

As it happened, these people were not so ungrateful.

"Sure, Raven," they called. "We remember you. We don't really need more light, not after this wonderful Moon you've already given us. But we're not the kind to reject the pleading of a brother."

So they gave him a huge pile of fish. Raven swallowed it down in short order.

"Very tasty, friends," cawed Raven. "You have my thanks. Now, cover your eyes, for here comes Sun."

Raven tore the bag open with his beak. Sharp points of light began shooting out in every direction. Then he caught the **pulsating** Sun in his beak and pulled it out of the bag. With a triumphant "Caw!" Raven flew into the sky and set Sun on its course.

The light was spectacular. It covered the world in a brilliant flush of color. The people fishing on the banks were amazed beyond words, as were the people fishing in canoes. Some were so startled that they leaped out of their canoes. Others on the river banks ran for the forests.

Those who leaped into the water became seals and otters and such. And those who ran to the forest became

---

[2] A clan is group of related families.

bears and badgers and the like. Only those who had been kind enough to feed Raven remained people.

Well, this was a very special moment, when Sun was set free. For what would the world be like without Sun? Sun made the trees and the plants grow tall and yield more fruits and nuts than before. Insects started to hum and buzz. Plants and animals began to cooperate with each other.

And fortunately, you and I are related to the people who gave Raven the fish. We can be thankful for that. For our ancestors grew stronger and braver ever afterwards. By the Sun's light, they could see how rich and wonderful the world really was. Many people even left their fishing nets and set out for distant places.

Raven was justly proud of all his doings. So he flew back to the Source. Raven called out for the Old One and his daughter—the one who was his mother when he was in his baby form.

"Mother, come and see!" cried Raven. "Come and see the world, now that I've set Sun free in the sky!"

"I see, son," said Raven's mother with fear in her voice. "And speaking for myself, I like everything you've done. But my father, the Old One, your grandfather, is very angry with you. He's tried for days to bring you back through magic. But now you've returned of your own free will, out of foolish pride. You'd better flee, for the Old One seeks revenge on you for the loss of his three prized bags."

"Pshaw, Mother!" said Raven with contempt. "I've done a good deed, and I won't apologize for it. Where is the Old One? I'll **confront** him and tell him so to his face."

So Raven boldly entered the Source House in search of the Old One. It was gloomy in that house without the glow of the bags hanging from the ceiling. The only remaining light came from some dying embers in the giant fireplace.

At last, Raven saw the Old One **sulking** by the fireplace. He was just sitting there, muttering the same words over and over in a kind of **incantation.** It was all rather frightening.

Hearing someone approach, the Old One turned and squinted into the gloom. "Who comes here?" he exclaimed. "Answer me now!"

"It is Raven who comes," whispered Raven. "It is the grandson of the Old One who comes. It is Raven who comes."

Old One stood up slowly in a rage.

"Raven, you're a **scoundrel,** and no kin of mine. You're the One Who Stole the Sun! The One Who Sets Things *Wrong!* Live with that name, if you will. But don't call yourself my grandson!"

"Silly Old One," said Raven quietly. "Just come and let me show you what I've done. Let me show you what Sun has done for people. Come."

"I'll show you what *I* can do!" said Old One. "Me, the Old One at the Source!"

With those words, the Old One took off his magical hat and twisted it until water spurted out the top. A pool of water formed on the floor.

"Is this supposed to scare me, Old One?" laughed Raven. "Water on the floor? It reminds me of when I used to wet myself as a baby. Ha! Caw! Caw! Caw!"

"Laugh if you will!" hissed Old One. "But look and beware! Beware!"

The Old One touched his magical hat again, and the water began to gush faster. Soon the house was flooded, and Raven and his mother had to climb to higher levels.

But as the house was flooding, so was the world. Water covered everything. The Old One was, after all, the Source of All Things. And all the rivers responded to his bidding.

People and animals huddled on the very tops of mountains, trying to save themselves from the floods of waters. It was a bad development for Raven and for the people he had tried to help.

Raven knew he had to act. So he changed his **dis-**

**traught** mother into a silver fish so she could swim away. Then Raven flew out through his old escape route—the smoke hole.

The world below him was drenched far and wide. His feathers were lashed by driving rain. It would not let up. Raven looked for people everywhere. He wanted to save them.

Finally he came to the highest mountaintop. There the animals were howling and growling in fear. But Raven heard the cries of children too. As it happened, only four children survived the flood. And it was these four children whose whimpering Raven heard.

So Raven flew close to the mountain and picked up the four children in his claws. Then he flew straight up to the ceiling of the sky. He pecked through the sky with his strong beak and held on. There he waited, sheltering the four children with his wings. Finally, the **persistent** rains stopped.

Then Raven let loose of the sky and flew lower in the clouds. He called for his old friend, Frog. Raven gently dropped the four children on Frog's green, soft back.

"Keep these children, Frog, until the waters **recede**," ordered Raven.

Frog kept them on her back for 20 long days. Finally, Frog saw that the waters were low enough and **coaxed** the children into wading to the shore.

Raven continued to fly over the earth. Raven's sharp eyes watched over everything. He checked on his mother, Silver Fish. And he watched over the four children as they grew older. He wasn't happy until he saw the people building villages again. Then he knew that people would once again fill the world.

When you see him today, don't think he's looking only for food. Raven's always hungry, to be sure. But food is only one of the many things he yearns for. He also wants to make the world better for all of us. He really is the One Who Sets Things Right—or tries to be!

# INSIGHTS

**A**long with most of the Native American groups of the Pacific Northwest, the Tlingit developed complex societies based on several social classes. The class order included the chief, nobility, common people (or workers), and slaves. Slaves were usually captives from other tribes or clans.

This class order was maintained through the use of a ceremony called the *potlatch*. As traditionally practiced, the potlatch was a feast and gift-giving ceremony in which people of high status displayed and shared their wealth.

Even though the rigid class structure is gone, the potlatch is still common today. Births, deaths, and even the building of a new house all provide opportunities for a potlatch ceremony. These ceremonies include feasting, singing, and dancing. They last from one day to several days. They might even last until the ceremonial food supply runs out.

When guests from a neighboring village are present at a potlatch, they are required to perform. While the guests sing or dance, the hosts watch carefully for insults. These insults can take the form of a song sung incorrectly or a mistake made in dancing. Likewise, the guests watch the hosts for any offense against them. If an insult occurs, fights might break out.

The Tlingit are well known for their art. They are highly skilled at wood carving, basket weaving, and pottery. Their cedar totem poles are very famous. These poles are carved and painted with figures of birds, animals, and fish. Sometimes they stand more than 80 feet tall. The Tlingit also create beautiful masks used for religious rituals.

The Tlingit are also fine crafters of canoes. They build canoes of all different sizes. The smallest vessel will seat two or three people. The largest can seat 60 people or more.

Among many Native American peoples, religious leaders were called shamans. As practiced among the Tlingit, the shaman communicated with village spirits and led ceremonies in their honor. Shamans also knew which herbs and animals were important in healing.

Many tribes still have a shaman. Some Native Americans send for a shaman *and* a medical doctor when they are ill.

According to traditional Tlingit belief, childbearing in a mother's home was forbidden—it was supposed to bring bad luck to the men of the house. So the pregnant woman gave birth in a small shelter built against the side of the house or nearby.

The Tlingit had an interesting way to keep a newborn baby from crying constantly. The first cry was captured in a container and sealed tight. The container was then buried in a place where many people walked. In this way the cry was smothered as the baby grew.

In the old days, the Tlingit lived in large wooden houses, usually containing around 30 occupants. A mother's oldest brother was named Keeper of the House. He stepped in when quarrels arose and dealt with other household concerns.

The Keeper of the House was highly respected. He was given the best food in the house. And he never performed housework. Another duty of the Keeper was to represent his house in the village ceremonies.

The traditional death ritual for the Tlingit offered another opportunity for a gathering. When a Tlingit died, the

*continued*

relatives placed the body in the back of the house in a sitting position. The body remained there for four days or more, while relatives feasted and sang.

Then a hole was made in a wall by removing a board. Before the body was removed through this hole, a dog was thrown through it. This was said to drive evil from the house.

Then the body was placed on a pile of logs and burned. The ashes were put in a small box and put away, sometimes in a place called a grave house.

# HOW AND WHY

## The Vision Quest
## Coyote and Death

**W**hat is the origin of corn? Why do people die?

Humans have asked questions like these since the beginning of time. And people have often looked to mythology for answers.

The following stories not only provide interesting answers to these questions. They also reveal the wisdom and humor of the Native American people who tell the stories.

# THE VISION QUEST

## VOCABULARY PREVIEW

Below is a list of words that appear in the story. Read the list and get to know the words before you read the story.

**benefit**—good
**(in) earnest**—serious
**expire**—die; pass away
**fatigue**—exhaustion; weakness
**meditate**—think; ponder
**nonchalantly**—calmly; effortlessly
**ominous**—threatening
**outmaneuvered**—overcome by greater skill
**perpetual**—constant
**plea**—request; appeal
**plumes**—feathers
**prevailing**—gaining the upper hand; triumphing
**resolved**—determined
**selfless**—unselfish
**tended**—watched over; cared for

## Main Characters

**Spirit youth**—spirit Wunzh meets in wilderness
**Wunzh**—young man
**Wunzh's father**—poor man of village

## The Scene

The action takes place in the wilderness outside a Chippewa village.

# The Vision Quest

*Many young men have searched for their guardian spirit. But these spirits are not easy to find. And when Wunzh thinks he has found his own, he discovers that his task is by no means over.*

**W**unzh[1] walked alone among birch trees and scrub willows beside a lake. The spring sun had long since reached its highest point and was quickly sinking.

[1] (woonz)

The boy heard a rustling in the brush nearby. Hope surged through him. Maybe this was the creature he was looking for. Wunzh stood quiet and still as a rabbit came hopping out of the grove of birch trees.

"Is it you?" Wunzh asked the rabbit under his breath.

The creature looked up but made no reply. The rabbit just **nonchalantly** hopped away into the grove.

"No, not you," muttered the boy. Wunzh felt discouraged. He had been walking all day in the woods that skirted his village. He questioned every creature that came along and many of the trees and plants. He asked a squirrel and a robin and several other rabbits. He asked an oak tree and a thorn bush. But Wunzh never heard the answer he wanted.

Now the boy continued making his way deeper into the woods. As he moved away from the open lake, he noticed that the light was already growing dim beneath the trees.

For a moment, he saw a dark shadow moving along nearby. Surely that was a bear, or maybe even a mountain lion. Wunzh stood frozen in place, torn between fear and hope.

"Is it you?" Wunzh whispered to the shadow. But there was no reply, and the creature faded away into the trees.

Wunzh looked around to see what he might have missed. Surely something in this forest would give him the reply he wanted.

"Is it you?" he asked a white-barked birch that grew apart from a dense grove. But there was no response. Nothing.

The boy turned and walked up a small hill. As he climbed, Wunzh thought back to that morning. He remembered the words his father had spoken to him. He could almost hear those words again.

"There comes a time," his father had said, "when every Chippewa boy becomes a man. This is when the boy finds out his purpose in life. Your time has come. You must seek your guardian spirit in a vision quest."

"How will I recognize my guardian spirit?" Wunzh had asked.

"There is no telling how the spirit will speak to you," replied his father. "Every person's quest is different. You must follow your own heart."

Then his father looked away in shame. "It is customary among our people for the father to build a lodge for his son," he said. "The boy would seek his vision there in privacy. But times are hard for our people. You will have to seek your vision in the wilderness."

The father pointed to the rolling hills and forests that surrounded the village. "You must walk until you find the right place," said the father. "You will recognize the spot, for something will speak to you."

Now the boy continued up the hill. He wished he could ask his father again, "How will I recognize my guardian spirit? How will I know where to look?"

At the top of the hill, Wunzh came to a clearing in the woods. From there he could watch the sun setting over the lake country. The orange light was just disappearing over the farthest hill.

As the boy stood there, a strange feeling swept over him. He suddenly knew that this was the right spot—even though he couldn't say why.

The boy sat down and began to **meditate.** Again, he remembered his father's advice.

"To seek out your guardian spirit," his father had said, "you must listen to your own spirit. Forget your body's demands for food and water. The body must bow to the spirit within."

Wunzh fell asleep with these words running through his mind.

The following day, Wunzh ate nothing. He felt his stomach tighten, and he began to feel weak. But he didn't give up.

Wunzh watched the animals and plants around him. He saw a hawk circle high above. Shadows from an oak tree shifted as the sun moved across the sky. But still he learned nothing.

Then Wunzh began to think about his people.

"Why must my people work so hard for their food and for their clothing?" Wunzh asked himself. "Why does my own family lack so many of the things that could give us comfort?

"We live like the wolves," Wunzh thought. "Our fathers hunt deer and rabbits and quail. The young men trap raccoons and muskrats. Others of our people spear or net fish.

"Even so, we're always hungry!" the boy exclaimed aloud. "Always hunting. Always trapping. Always fishing. Always searching for roots and the berries that grow among the brambles. Yet we're still hungry!"

Wunzh fell asleep with his mind full of such thoughts, still thinking of the **perpetual** struggle for food his people faced. So it happened that Wunzh had an unusual dream.

He dreamed that he was visited by a strange and marvelous youth. The handsome boy was yellow-green in color. His head was crowned with long and waving green and yellow **plumes** that reached high into the sky. The youth was quite tall, but the waving feathers made him look like a giant.

"Rise and wrestle me, boy of the Chippewa," said the spirit.

These were strange words of challenge to Wunzh's ears. He was not without fear, for this fellow was two or three times as large as he was. And his waving plumes made him look **ominous** indeed.

"Are you my guardian spirit?" asked Wunzh directly. "Are you the vision that I seek?"

"I heard your **plea** for your people," answered the spirit. "You seek **benefit** not just for yourself, or even just for your family. You seek good for all. So I've come to assist you. But first you must wrestle me."

Wunzh was puzzled. "Why must I wrestle you?" he asked. "I seek a vision, not competition."

"You'll understand in due time," said the strange youth. "Now stand up and defend yourself."

It's not easy to wrestle when you've had no food and water for a whole day. Wunzh felt weak and tired, but he accepted the spirit's challenge.

They wrestled hard. Wunzh seized the spirit's arm, pulled it behind him, and forced the spirit face down to the ground. But the spirit slipped out of Wunzh's grasp and pinned Wunzh down in the same manner.

Time after time, Wunzh would find himself on the verge of victory, only to be **outmaneuvered** by the spirit. Wunzh had indeed found a powerful opponent. Then, just as Wunzh was about to pass out from **fatigue,** the spirit vanished.

When Wunzh awoke the next day, he was puzzled. The green boy had not claimed to be his guardian.

"Besides that," Wunzh thought, "he sure didn't look like any plant or animal I've ever seen before."

But Wunzh reminded himself how powerful the spirit had been. And whatever the green boy was, he had said he would bring help. So Wunzh stayed in his place and continued his fast.

That night the strange youth returned. He again ordered Wunzh to wrestle him. Again, Wunzh and the spirit took turns **prevailing** over one another. Then, at the moment when Wunzh felt himself collapsing, the spirit disappeared into the night air of Wunzh's dreams.

"Surely this must be my protector, my guardian spirit," said Wunzh aloud. "But he hasn't said so. I don't understand what's going on."

All the same, Wunzh stayed in his place.

The next day, Wunzh continued his fast. He figured that he would have to wrestle the green boy again that night. But he was growing weaker from his lack of food and water.

"I don't know how much longer I can keep this up," Wunzh muttered to a passing robin. But the bird made no answer.

On the third night, the spirit returned and wrestled with Wunzh again. They struggled with one another as before, and neither prevailed. But this time, the green boy did not just disappear. This time, the plumed spirit stayed and spoke to Wunzh.

"When I return tomorrow night, it will be for the last time," said the spirit. "It will be our final wrestling match. And in that match, you will defeat me."

"That's impossible!" exclaimed Wunzh. "I can hardly move, much less wrestle. See how weak my arms are! I can't possibly defeat you."

"Nonetheless, you will do it," responded the spirit. "Not only that, but you will kill me."

"I wouldn't dare!" exclaimed Wunzh. "You're my protector—aren't you?"

"You must, for I demand it," continued the spirit calmly. "When I'm dead, take off all my clothes and bury me in a grave which you must dig yourself. Make my grave just right—not too deep and not too shallow.

"Now pay special attention, for this is important," added the spirit firmly. "Bury me where the sun will hit my grave. Take care of my grave each day. For as the days pass, weeds will try to take over. But you must keep my grave clear so that the sun can shine on it."

"Why must I do these things?" asked Wunzh.

"Soon enough, you'll understand," said the spirit. With these mysterious words, the spirit disappeared.

Wunzh began to doubt himself. "Perhaps this spirit isn't my protector at all," Wunzh worried to himself. "Perhaps I should return home for food."

Wunzh shook himself. "I must guard against such thoughts," he said to himself. "I'll wait for the spirit's return. I must not give in to my body's demands."

That morning, Wunzh was awakened by his father. "My son, you've been out here for a week. Look at you. You're just about wasted away from fasting. Here, eat some food and return home with me. It's time."

Wunzh was tempted by the food, for he was very

hungry indeed. But he was **resolved** to stay one more night—to wrestle one last time with the plumed spirit. He had to find out for himself what the outcome would be. He had to find out if this strange green boy was truly his protector. And most of all, Wunzh had to find out if he could really get help for his people.

"No, Father," Wunzh said. "I will stay for another day. Then I'll return. It's important, Father."

Wunzh's father realized that Wunzh was in **earnest.** His son's quest was about to be realized.

"I understand," said his father. "My blessings are with you, my son." So Wunzh's father left and returned home alone.

The next evening, just at sunset, the spirit youth returned. This time, Wunzh couldn't tell whether he was dreaming or awake. It all seemed the same to him now.

"Are you ready?" the spirit youth asked.

"As ready as I'll ever be," replied Wunzh weakly. Indeed, he wondered if he could even stand, much less wrestle and kill the green boy.

"This will be our last meeting," warned the spirit. "Do you remember what I said last night?"

"I remember," came the reply.

The next moment, the two were wrestling with all their might. They struggled equally for a while, one pinning the other by turns. But Wunzh felt himself weakening and knew he could not hold out for long. Then, just when Wunzh was about to breathe his very last and **expire,** the spirit of the green boy died.

Wunzh stood back, gasping for breath. He couldn't believe that he had won. But rather than a thrill of victory, Wunzh felt a great sadness. He had grown to admire the spirit boy. And Wunzh hadn't really believed that he could kill a being so powerful.

And yet Wunzh felt that what he had done was somehow right. So far, he had followed exactly the instructions of his guardian spirit. But now he had more details to take care of. So respectfully, yet sadly, Wunzh carried out all the spirit's burial instructions to the very last letter. Then he walked home.

The people in the poor village noticed that Wunzh had changed. He wore a more serious face, and he spent more time alone. But Wunzh refused to talk about his vision quest. His family and the people in the village respected his silence, even though they were filled with curiosity.

Wunzh knew his task was not yet over. Each and every day he visited the grave and **tended** it as the spirit had instructed. Days passed. Weeks passed. Then Wunzh saw a marvelous thing. Thin, yellowish-green spikes of grass began to push up through the earth of the grave.

Each day, these little spikes grew taller, until central stalks formed. Long, pointed leaves grew out from these central stalks. Then, as if by magic, tassels began to form.

"These tassels make the plants seem taller," said Wunzh to himself. "Just like the spirit wrestler."

All through the rest of the spring and summer, Wunzh took care of the plants. Then, in the late summer, the young man called his father. "Come see what I have cared for," he said. "I have followed my vision to this very day. And these fine plants are the result.

"Look at these tassels and the many seeds they contain," continued Wunzh. "I have tasted these seeds. They are delicious and life-giving."

"Where did these plants come from?" asked Wunzh's father. "I have never seen anything like them."

"I wrestled and killed a green spirit who appeared to me," Wunzh explained. "Before he died, the spirit told me to bury him here. But I wasn't sure what to expect. I wasn't sure if he was a friendly spirit or an evil vision. It appears that he *was* my guardian spirit, after all."

"No, son," said Wunzh's father. "The spirit wrestler was the guardian spirit of *all* our people. Now the Chippewa won't have to depend on wild berries and hunted animals. We can grow these plants to help feed the people."

Wunzh's father was very proud of his son. For his quest had been **selfless** and generous. And its fruit would help people in all four directions of the wind. So it was that Wunzh, through his noble efforts, helped bring corn to his people.

To this day, long rows of corn grow high. And every now and then, when golden-green tassels reach toward the sky, Corn Spirit remembers wrestling Wunzh. Then the guardian spirit smiles.

# INSIGHTS

The Chippewa—also called the Ojibway—were once part of the Algonquin peoples of the northeast. But due to droughts and conflicts with European settlers, they migrated west. They settled in the forest country around the shores of Lake Superior.

The traditional Chippewa were skilled in fishing and hunting. But grains such as rice and corn were important parts of their diet as well.

Tobacco—even today—is a sacred substance to the Chippewa. Many meetings and ceremonies begin with the smoking of tobacco in a special pipe.

The ceremonial pipe was also used when a new chief came to power. Tribal elders were responsible for selecting new leaders. When they chose someone, they offered him the pipe. If that person smoked the pipe, it meant he accepted the position of chief.

The Chippewa style of leadership was quite different from the European style. Usually the chief didn't make decisions alone. Rather, important matters were discussed in a council. All adult men and women were invited to this council and either approved or disapproved the chief's proposed action.

The chiefs were civil chiefs. This meant that they ruled during peacetime. But when it became necessary to fight a battle, a self-appointed war chief took over.

A war chief could hold power just as long as a war lasted—and then only if the people supported him. A war chief's followers would leave him if he lost too many battles.

The Ojibway were not fond of war. They believed it a poor—and dangerous—way of showing courage and strength. Only in times of great crisis did they smoke the War Pipe.

According to traditional Chippewa belief, the power to heal wasn't learned. People who had the gift of healing were looked for carefully. Such individuals were invited by the medicine men and women—called Mide—to join the Grand Medicine Society.

The Mide used their knowledge of herbs and plants to heal sickness. The Grand Medicine Society also promoted the vision quest—such as the one you read about in the myth. They taught that such quests were healthy for the mind and body.

Traditional Chippewa burial practices reveal some of their beliefs of the afterlife. The body of a dead person was laid out for four days. This gave enough time for the spirit to leave the corpse and travel to the underworld.

After four days, the body was wrapped in the bark of a birch tree and buried. Often the Chippewa built a small wooden house over the grave.

The family of a dead Chippewa mourned for a year after the death. When the year was up, they held a feast. At the celebration a place was set for the dead person— to show that the dead remain in the family forever.

Today there are Chippewa reservations scattered from Michigan to the Dakotas. Some of the major ones are Turtle Mountain, Red Lake, White Earth, and Greater Leech Lake in Minnesota. Chippewa reservations in Wisconsin include Lac du Flambeau and Lac Courte Oreilles. The Chippewas are the second largest group of Native Americans in the United States.

# COYOTE AND DEATH

# VOCABULARY PREVIEW

Below is a list of words that appear in the story. Read the list and get to know the words before you read the story.

**adeptly**—ably; skillfully
**assent**—agreement
**assurance**—confidence; firmness
**encountered**—met; came across
**fabrication**—made-up story
**far-fetched**—unlikely; unbelievable
**hypocrite**—false person
**imposing**—impressive; important-looking
**lair**—den
**modify**—change a little; adjust
**mourners**—those saddened by the death of a loved one
**rejection**—being turned down
**skeptical**—suspicious; doubting
**tirades**—angry speeches
**wrath**—anger

## Main Characters

**Coyote**—trickster
**Great Shaman**—medicine man

## The Scene

The action takes place before death entered the world.

# Coyote
# and Death

*At one time, Death didn't take
people and animals away to his
land. But Coyote changed all that.
He wanted more room to move
about. And he thought Death
could give it to him. Coyote got
space to move, all right—more
space than he bargained for.*

**C**oyote always liked wide-open spaces. He loved the
freedom to roam around, undisturbed by other creatures.
That was Coyote's nature.

It was also Coyote's way to let everyone know if anything bothered him. So it's not surprising that he made a
fuss when he noticed that the world was becoming rather

crowded. Coyote decided that there were too many people and animals in the world. And in his usual fashion, Coyote started griping to anyone who would listen.

"I need some elbow room," growled Coyote to a man he met on a trail. "Why do I bump into people everywhere I go?"

"Why can't we do something to decrease this overcrowding?" Coyote demanded of a flock of geese on the shore of a lake. "I can't even get to the water with you creatures all over the place."

"Why not, say, throw away the old ones?" Coyote asked a large family that all lived together. "Maybe they could just be done away with. I know it would be better for me. I like my space."

Usually, all the people and animals just ignored Coyote's questions and suggestions. After all, he was always complaining about something. That was what it meant to be Coyote. Besides, everyone knew that Coyote was a troublemaker.

But Coyote wouldn't give up. Every time he met someone, he'd start in again.

"Listen, I've got an idea," Coyote would say. "It would be better for all of us if those who have been here for a long time would just *die*. Don't you agree?"

Coyote ran all over the prairie shouting about his proposal. He shouted his plan so loudly that it was heard in the faraway forest and the distant desert. Now most of those who heard didn't pay it much mind. They were used to Coyote's **tirades.** Besides, they didn't know what it meant to die.

But that winter it snowed hard and often. The drifts grew higher than anyone had ever seen. It became almost impossible to use the trails and paths. Everyone was cold and miserable. Food became very scarce. Is it any wonder that Coyote picked up his old familiar complaining again?

"This is a sad state of affairs," whined Coyote. "I'm hungry. You're hungry. We're all hungry. There are just too many of us. It seems to me that the oldest among us should say farewell and leave this life behind. Then we'd all have enough food to eat."

Now, there lived a very powerful person in those parts. Everyone called him Great Shaman.[1] He had always ignored Coyote, like everyone else did at first. But now he'd had enough. Great Shaman had heard these same complaints over and over again, all winter long. And now he was beginning to hear them from his own people, not just from Coyote.

"Enough is enough," said Great Shaman. "This scoundrel must be punished for spreading such outrageous ideas."

Of course, Great Shaman was not a young man. He was getting up there in years. So perhaps Coyote's plan was especially disturbing to him. It hit close to home.

Great Shaman wanted to drive Coyote away and be rid of the whiner. But he knew that Coyote wasn't that easy to handle. Besides, Great Shaman was afraid that he might be accused of a conflict of interest. So he wisely called a meeting of all the people and animals. He would hold a great council, and the views and opinions of all could be heard.

Now a certain sacred rock was familiar to all, so everyone agreed to meet there. Great Shaman dressed in his most colorful clothes and his most **imposing** feathers and jewelry. He was commanding and awe-inspiring, standing on that big rock.

"Children, hear my voice," began Great Shaman. "Listen, all who see me here. Everything breathing and living, I asked you here to consider Coyote's proposal.

"You've all heard him yelping around here," continued the shaman. "You've heard him call for the old ones to go away and never return. Why, he wants some of you to die."

A murmur ran among the people.

"What does it mean, to 'die'?" one asked.

---

[1] A shaman is a religious leader who uses magic.

"I'm not sure," another replied. "I think it means to go away and never come back."

"How dreadful!" observed yet another.

After Great Shaman allowed the people and animals to talk for a short while, he again began to speak. Everyone grew silent and listened to him.

"Now I want you to speak directly to Coyote," said Great Shaman. "I want you to tell him just what you think of his plan. My hope is that you'll say 'no' to his ideas. Let's teach Coyote a good and final lesson."

All the people and animals began to talk with each other again. They discussed the pros and cons of Coyote's plan. What did it really mean, they wondered. Who would it affect?

All this time, Coyote sat a healthy distance from the sacred rock. He sat scratching behind his left ear, trying to look unconcerned. But he could hear the murmurs of the crowd. He could see them glancing his way from time to time, usually frowning. It was pretty obvious to him that he might be in for a disappointment.

Of course, Coyote was used to **rejection.** But he was also used to thinking on his feet. Quick thinking was how he survived. It was clear to him that he had to **modify** his proposal a bit.

So Coyote stood up and cleared his throat and asked for a minute to say a few words.

"Great Shaman and good friends here on this earth," said Coyote slyly, "perhaps you don't fully understand my plan. I don't want to harm anyone. I seek only to help out. You know that is my way."

"Sure, sure" said the people in disbelief. "We've heard *that* before!"

"But it's true!" protested Coyote defensively. "I really *am* always trying to help out. It's just that there isn't enough food for all of us. Surely you agree that we're always hungry. We're hungry in the morning when the sun rises. And at noon when the sun is on high. And in the evening when the sun is sinking. Whether our shadows are large or small, we are always hungry. Is it not so?"

The crowd began to nod their heads and murmur **assent.** Of course, this was just what Coyote was waiting for. He stepped closer.

"When I proposed that the old ones go away," Coyote said, "I never meant to suggest that they couldn't return. In my plan, people and animals can die for a while and then come back again. I had in mind something like a long nap or a vacation. You go for a while, then you return. We can all take turns."

"How is your plan going to work?" asked Squirrel. "Where will the dead people and animals go?"

"Do you really want to hear?" asked Coyote with anger in his voice. "Are you sincere in asking? Because *I'm* certainly sincere. I don't like being regarded a trouble-maker. You've all been acting like I'm not worth listening to."

"Oh, go ahead and tell us the details," said the people. "Don't be so sensitive. Just tell us. But make it snappy."

Even Great Shaman leaned forward to listen.

"Well... okay," began Coyote. "Here's what I have in mind. We would make a hole in the sky, up there in heaven. Then the dead could enter through that hole. After their stay in the sky, they could come back the same way. It's as simple as that."

Coyote raised one eyebrow and glanced around the crowd to see who was buying this line. He could always sell a bill of goods, you know. His tongue was not only long, it was smooth too.

Bear was **skeptical.** "I know my trees, and I've climbed some tall ones in my day," drawled Bear. "But I've never **encountered** a tree that tall—not one that would get you to the sky. And that hole you're talking about—I don't see how you'd get up there."

Bear was like that—practical.

"It would take a giant tree, Bear," stammered Coyote. "But you're right, that wouldn't work. Ah... what it would take... is a... an... an arrow, a special arrow. Ah, yes, an arrow, that's what I have in mind."

Of course, Coyote was making this up as he went along. He's a natural storyteller.

"We'll shoot an arrow into the sky, you see," continued Coyote quickly. "Then we'll shoot a second arrow into that one, and so on until we have a chain of arrows reaching all the way from the sky to the ground. It'll be a snap—as easy as the twang of a bowstring."

You could almost see Coyote trembling throughout this chapter of his **fabrication.** But the people and the animals seemed to be buying it. Even Great Shaman was shaking his head in agreement. True, it seemed pretty **far-fetched.** But what better idea was there?

Even Bear agreed. And he was the most skeptical one present. Badger, too, thought it might work. He had been without food for many days, and hunger was affecting his logic.

"Go ahead and try it," everyone agreed.

Coyote's fast talking had worked. The people and animals scurried about importantly. The people carefully selected the most powerful bows and the straightest arrows. The animals helped choose a dozen archers with good aim and strong arms. Finally all was ready.

Since it was his project, Coyote gave the signal. "Ready, aim, SHOOT!"

A dozen arrows were shot one right after the other. The first one hit the sky and stuck. Then the next arrow hit the first one. The archers kept shooting until a chain of arrows hung from the sky. Even Coyote stood looking up in disbelief. He really hadn't expected it to work. But he didn't dare show his amazement.

A chain of arrows now reached from the sky down to the sacred rock. The Great Shaman rose and pulled at the arrows with all of his might. They held. He pulled again, this time with both hands. Again the arrows held. The arrow chain was very strong.

"The deed is done," spoke Great Shaman. "We've created a pathway to the sky world.

"Return to your homes," continued the holy man. "When night falls, Death will walk down the arrow path."

"What will happen then?" asked the Badger.

"I suppose Death will choose some of us to take back with him," said Great Shaman with a glance at Coyote. "Of course, those chosen will live in the sky home for just a time. Then they'll return to us again. That's the plan, isn't it, Coyote?"

"Yes, yes," said Coyote, his voice full of **assurance.**

That night Death did descend the arrow pathway. And he did pick several animals and people to take back with him to the sky world. He took Badger with him, and Eagle, and Lion. He took Spider and Rat as well. He took a hunter from his fireside. And he took a small girl-child from her play.

Death led his new companions to the sacred rock and lifted them up the arrow path to the sky world.

The next morning, everyone gathered at the sacred rock to see who was missing. Immediately the people and animals left on the earth began to wait for the return of those Death had taken. Every day they looked at the arrow path. But no one returned.

"Where are they?" grumbled the people. "Coyote promised that they would be able to visit whenever they wanted to."

As for Coyote, he took to his **lair** and didn't come out for days. And the longer Coyote remained in hiding, the more suspicious the people became.

"That rascal Coyote has tricked us again!" shouted Bear. "Our friends aren't coming back. Coyote just wants to have more room and food for himself."

"Let's be patient a little longer," advised Great Shaman. "But if our friends don't return soon, we'll go have a little talk with Coyote."

The people and animals waited and waited. But their friends didn't return. Finally they went to find Coyote. But when they went to his den, they couldn't get him to come out. They heard a strange grinding noise coming from inside the den.

"What is that strange noise?" asked Bear.

"Maybe he is crying over the failure of his plan," answered Rabbit.

"Most likely, Coyote is up to no good," said Great Shaman. "Let's just leave him alone."

But Coyote was actually grinding his teeth, trying to make them sharper. Had the animals and people known what he was up to, they would have been horrified. He'd come up with yet another plan—one that would make absolutely certain that the dead would never return to earth.

One night at midnight, Coyote sneaked to the sacred rock. He crept along very softly and quietly on his padded feet. When he reached the rock, he grabbed the arrow ladder with his teeth. He began to gnaw at the bottom arrow.

"There must be a way to do away with this pathway," said Coyote to himself. "I certainly don't want all the dead to come back."

Then Coyote realized that he would never chew through the arrow. So he shook the arrow wildly, moving his head frantically from one side to the next. Then he felt the chain of arrows give. All of the arrows came tumbling down from the sky.

"Success!" barked Coyote.

Coyote had destroyed the very pathway he had so **adeptly** designed. But his moment of victory was short. For some of the falling arrows stuck in Coyote's back.

"Ahooooo! Ahooooo!" howled Coyote. He ran wildly back to his den, trying to pull the stinging arrows out of his hide.

Coyote's howling awakened Great Shaman and all of the other **mourners.** When they saw what Coyote had done, a great feeling of despair entered their hearts.

"See!" cried Bear. "Now the dead will never be able to return home."

Great Shaman snapped into action. He had never

been so angry, and his **wrath** was swift and harsh.

"Coyote, you villain!" shouted Great Shaman. "We listened to you. We believed you. You've betrayed our trust. And you had the nerve to talk about sincerity! What a **hypocrite** you are!

"For your dishonesty," continued Great Shaman, "I banish you from our midst. You must go into the prairie and never return. You brought Death among us and made sure our dead ones could never return. So it shall be with you. You, too, must go away and never return.

"Do your mischief as you will. But do it away from us," continued Shaman. "Your wish has come true. You will have all the open space you want out there all by yourself. And much loneliness. Now go!"

Coyote heard his sentence, and it hurt more than the sky arrows stuck in his back. It hurt even more than the hunger in his stomach.

Coyote turned and trotted to the west. Every so often, he looked back, his long tongue hanging out the side of his mouth and his tail drooping low between his legs. He trotted for several days. And the farther he went, the more he regretted his mischief.

That night he stopped and looked up at the full moon. He thought he saw some of the ghosts of the people he had banished to Death's land. A feeling of loneliness and fear swept over him. Coyote raised his head to the moon and howled.

"Howl, howl, howl! Howl, howl, howl! Ahooooo, ahooooo!"

To this day, you can hear Coyote howl at the moon. And when you do, you'll know just how he feels about loneliness and death.

# INSIGHTS

**A**n old Caddo legend tells how the first people came out of an underground cave to live on earth. But before all the people were out, a wolf sealed the entrance. The people on earth waited, but they soon realized those left behind would be underground forever. And—according to this story—people who die go back under the earth and are united with those forgotten people.

Caddo lodges were very large and held about eight to ten families. The buildings almost always had several entrances—but not because there were so many people.

The doors on the north and south were usually kept tightly shut. They were only used during certain ceremonies.

And use of the east and west entrances depended on the location of the sun. The Caddo adored the sun and wanted it to be the first or last thing they saw as they left or entered their lodge. So the east entrance was used in the morning, as the sun was rising. The west door was used in the evening when the sun was setting.

The sun also played an important part in the birth of a baby. When a child was born it was placed in the east doorway before the rising sun. The Caddo believed the sun would see the child and give it a special blessing.

The Caddo protected their youngsters in another way. After a baby was born, a bright fire was started. It was kept burning for ten days and nights to keep evil away from the baby.

After the tenth day, the fire was allowed to smoulder. But it wasn't put out completely until the child was two years old.

The evils the Caddo feared for their young children were frightening indeed. There were winged animals that could eat people, especially babies. There were also the mythical cannibal people. These people looked like anyone else. But at night they stole human children to eat.

These evil creatures worked only in the darkness. This is why Caddoes kept their fires burning—the light kept the evils away.

In the summer the Caddo spent most of their time outdoors—farming, hunting, fishing, and building new lodges. When colder weather arrived, they rarely left their cabins. Instead, they stayed indoors making bows and arrows, reed mats, and pottery. They also told stories around the fire.

During hunting season, many villagers got together in groups of ten to twenty. These groups spread out over a wide area to hunt. A long hunting expedition could last several months and could cover hundreds of miles.

The Caddo originally settled on the Red River in Louisiana, where they remained for hundreds of years. Gradually they moved westward. Today most Caddo live in a region that includes parts of four states—Louisiana, Texas, Arkansas, and Oklahoma.